SHW

APR 1 0 1995

Zero Proof

200 Nonalcoholic Drinks from America's
Most Famous Bars
and Restaurants

Pamela Stovall &
Richard Lalich

ST. MARTIN'S PRESS
NEW YORK

To Dorie, still my friend and mother. To Howard, even though it's only a second book. And to my favorite bartender, Rick Leonardo, who with our friendship has truly experienced a mix of sweet and sour ... but never on the rocks.

—P. S.

For Margaret

Portions of this book first appeared in *Playboy* magazine in a slightly different form.

Library of Congress Cataloging-in-Publication Data

Stovall, Pamela.
    Zero proof / Pamela Stovall and Richard Lalich.
        p.   cm.
    ISBN 0-312-11479-6
    1. Beverages.   2. Cocktails.   I. Lalich, Richard.   II. Title.
TX815.S83   1994
641.8′75—dc20   94-22235
                                                                      CIP

First Edition: November 1994

10 9 8 7 6 5 4 3 2 1

Contents

Acknowledgments

We would like to thank the owners, managers, and bartenders at the bars, clubs, hotels, resorts, and restaurants who talked with us about this book.

We would also like to thank our St. Martin's Press editor, Barbara Anderson, and assistant editor, Marian Lizzi.

And our thanks to our agent, Sandy Choron of March Tenth, who got us into this mess. Also ...

... Thanks to the people who offered ideas and support: Naomi Sparks and Al Kaiser; Craig and Michele Baranowski; Ed Sickinger; Paul Kish; Eleanor Morris; Linda Walters; Julia and the late Adrian Geldhof; Bea and Jack Russell; Annie and Mary Moerdyk; Jim and Loraine Christians; Peg and Joe Leonardo; Shirley (Grabill) VanderVeen; Jack and Ruth Christians; Alan and Sue Geldhof; Velma Holben; Bill Preston and Doris Gillis; the crazy Keelcos; Michael Conlin; Anna Maria Clark; Howard, Audry, and Allison Stovall; Phil, Debbie, Emily, and Sarah Sweeney; Kim and Donna Jean Preston; and the most bizarre Dennis Stovall.   —P. S.

... Grateful acknowledgment is due the following people for their support, ideas, and patience: John Rezek, to whose brilliant inspiration for the *Playboy* article and usual superb guidance I owe my original interest in this subject; Margaret Lalich, whom we both agree is my much better half; Phyllis Tarczueski, who sparkles; Sue Basinger; Jonathan Black; Robert Lalich; and (in alphabetical order) Diane Boyko, Rob Harris, Rich Hefter, Jan Parr, Gretchen Reynolds, Dennis Rodkin, Fred Rogers, Bill Savage, Dennis Tablizo, Carolyn Thur, and Bill Zehme, among others.   —R. L.

Introduction

You brake for cocktails. Your friends order drinks, and for a glum moment it seems that you'll be left out of the fun. Not long ago, the only recourse for a person who chose not to drink alcohol was to order a Shirley Temple, or to fidget with an unused cocktail napkin while his or her tablemates savored the serendipitous encounters of sour and sweet in a rocks glass.

But these days, there's no reason to feel excluded. The alternatives to alcohol are no longer as dull as club soda. America's best restaurants and bars now offer a tempting selection of nonalcoholic drinks for everyone who opts not to imbibe—the driver who chooses none for the road, the executive who wishes to remain clear-headed during a business engagement, the revelers who decide to supplement their consumption of alcohol with drinks that are alcohol-free. And a new, quickly growing group: people who order nonalcoholic drinks simply because they enjoy the exquisite flavors.

After all, there's no law that says liquorless drinks must be tame. Coffee, soft drinks, and water will get you through in a pinch, but they won't slake your thirst for adult drinks— drinks that look and taste like real cocktails. Exercising self-discipline and good judgment deserve to be rewarded. Fortunately, the new alcohol-free options offer more variety and better taste than you imagined.

Wines without alcohol surpass ordinary grape juices and ciders in that they mimic the experience of drinking authentic wines: the extraction of the cork, the aroma, the grapy hues, and that silky splash of wine against the inside of a wineglass.

Many alcohol-free brews provide the hoppy, bitter flavor of beer without the buzz, and more than seventy brands are now available—including versions of nearly every popular domestic and imported brand.

Until recently, one of the drawbacks to drinking responsibly was the absence of the trappings—a ginger ale in a short glass offers none of the visceral and tactile pleasures of the old lick-of-salt, chug-of-tequila, bit-of-lime ritual. Today's bartenders will serve zero-proof drinks in more traditional surroundings: a virgin daiquiri in a bubble glass, a pseudo pilsner in a beer mug, a fizzy cider poured into a champagne flute.

At Manhattan's '21' Club, bartender Will Higgins receives requests for freshly squeezed juices, mineral waters, and virgin versions of blender drinks. "It's not fashionable anymore to be seen bellying up to the bar for four or five hours," says Higgins. In Los Angeles, where taxis are scarce, drinking responsibly or not at all is a practical matter. "More and more people are telling me, 'No thanks, I'm the designated driver tonight,'" says Spago bartender Rob Thurman. Thurman adds, "A popular drink is cranberry juice mixed with soda, Pellegrino, or orange juice."

Bartenders, of course, know all about remaining sober while drinking in a bar. What do they pour for themselves while they pull ten-hour shifts in saloons? At Sage's Sages near Chicago, the drink of choice behind the bar is orange juice with a shot of soda—a recipe dubbed the B-Girl Cocktail in earlier days. At Spago, the staff nurses a nonalcoholic concoction called the Alligator. A satisfying mixture of lime juice, cassis, soda, and 7-Up, the Alligator has been a house secret for eleven years, and regular customers of the chic eatery have learned to ask for it.

Across the country, there's a new emphasis on providing delicious alternatives to alcohol. Today most bars and restaurants offer a nonalcoholic special that is exclusive to its establishment; the others apply a distinctive twist to familiar standbys often served alcohol-free, such as Virgin Marys, Daiquiris, and Piña Coladas. With this in mind, we asked

America's best restaurants, inns, and nightclubs to share their recipes for one or more of the nonalcoholic drinks that they serve to their patrons. Many of the recipes that follow are exclusive to the restaurants where they are served, and are printed here for the first time.

In all, we interviewed more than five hundred restaurant owners, bartenders, wine stewards, beverage managers, executive chefs, pastry chefs, bar managers, innkeepers, and maître d's to gather the recipes that follow. For the chapters that cover nonalcoholic beer and wine, we spoke with top executives, brand managers, or representatives of nearly every brewery and winery that makes nonalcoholic versions. We calculated the number of calories in each mixed drink by reading product labels and by quizzing the manufacturers of the ingredients.

Browse through the recipes, then mix a few—and you'll agree that these drinks rank with the best you'll find anywhere ... with or without alcohol. They're as refreshing as the Rosemary Lemonade at Vidalia, and as creative as the Cinnamon Twist at Kaspar's. They're as sophisticated as Casey's Special, available only at Sardi's Restaurant—and now, in your home; as sensually enjoyable as the best-selling drink at Planet Hollywood, a strawberry-banana smoothie called Home Alone; as low in calories as the Tropical Fruit Punch at Mark's Place; as rich as the Frozen Oreo Cookie enjoyed by patrons at Daisy Buchanan's saloon; and as exotic as the Tootsie Pop Shake served exclusively at Aspen's celebrated Restaurant at The Little Nell.

The drinks hail from America's pinnacles of fine dining— Stars, The Maisonette, the '21' Club, Sardi's, The Inn at Little Washington, Spago, and others—and from the places one simply must experience when visiting certain cities—Jake's Famous Crawfish Restaurant in Portland, San Francisco's Fog City Diner, Juanita's in Little Rock, The Fiddlehead in Juneau, Louie's Backyard in Key West, and The Mansion on Turtle Creek in Dallas. Others are from acclaimed new hot spots such as Daniel, Resto des Amis, and Bossa Nova, and famous nightclubs such as Antone's, CBGB, The House of Blues, Kingston Mines, and Second City.

How to Use This Book

We've divided the recipes into five chapters, based on the drink's main ingredients. The five categories are sodas and tonics; fruits and vegetable juices; frozen drinks; Virgin Bloody Marys; and after-dinner drinks, including coffee and ice cream drinks. You'll find the number of calories per serving at the end of each recipe.

We've made sure that just about every one of the ingredients in the recipes can be found in a bar, in your home, or on the shelf of a typical supermarket or liquor store. While the flavors are expansive, the preparation is not; in minutes, you can create a drink that is just as sublime as the ones served in world-class restaurants and bars. To ensure that you haven't overlooked any of the supplies you'll need, take a look at the chapter titled "Setting Up Your Own Nonalcoholic Bar."

You'll also find a chapter devoted to dealcoholized wine, and another that will brief you on the vastly improved nonalcoholic beers, and their surprisingly low calorie counts.

Finally, at the end of the book are two indexes: one lists all of the drinks alphabetically; the other, broken down by state and city, provides the addresses and phone numbers of the restaurants, hotels, resorts, and nightclubs that provided the recipes.

This book, then, can be used in two ways: as a guide that takes you through the steps to making delicious drinks at home, just as they're made at the best restaurants; and as a companion to planning your next business trip or vacation, to point you to places where you can be assured of imaginative nonalcoholic drink choices.

Of course, this book can be used in still another way. When the occasion calls for it, all of the recipes can be modified by adding modest amounts of alcohol. But the question is: Why would you want to?

A Note on Calories

All calorie counts for drinks are subject to variation, depending on the specific ingredients used. For example, fresh orange juice has a lower calorie content than canned or frozen juice. Also, the calories in mixes change with brands. For example, one ounce of Mr. & Mrs. T Bloody Mary mix contains 4.4 calories; one ounce of a similar Holland House Bloody Mary mixer contains 10 calories.

Zero
Proof

Simple and Sweet

Mixers, Tonics, and Rickeys

Spago
The Alligator

¼ shot cassis
½ shot lime juice
4 ounces club soda
4 ounces 7-Up

1. Fill a Collins glass with ice.
2. Pour ingredients into the Collins glass.
3. Mix well.

CALORIES: 68

Spago, Wolfgang Puck's glamorous eatery, has become nearly as celebrated as the Hollywood glitterati who hold court there. Actors, agents, and studio moguls make movie deals while supping on gorgeously presented entrées that are as light as an air kiss.

Dixie Belle Saloon
Rebel Yell
---

4 ounces 7-Up
4 ounces cranberry juice
1 lemon wedge
1 stemmed cherry

1. In a tumbler, pour 7-Up and cranberry juice.
2. Add ice.
3. Stir.
4. Garnish with lemon and cherry.

CALORIES: 122

When Madonna was still singing in the shower in Michigan, Dolly Parton grabbed her career by the throat and shook it till it gave her what she wanted. Big breasts and big hair helped, but that alone certainly wouldn't have taken her as far as she's gone, nor for as long. She's a woman who deserves her own theme park. Or two. The Dixie Belle Saloon is part of the Dixie Stampede Dinner attraction, owned by Parton's Dollywood entertainment park, with locations in Pigeon Forge, Tennessee, and Myrtle Beach, South Carolina. Feast on down-home favorites such as roasted chicken, hickory-smoked ribs, corn on the cob, and Dixie bread, while watching cowboys and cowgirls provide a spectacular display of horsemanship.

Sardi's Restaurant
Casey Special

3 ounces tonic
3 ounces seltzer water
1 liberal dash Angostura
bitters
1 lime slice

1. Fill a highball glass with ice.
2. Add equal parts tonic and seltzer.
3. Shake in a liberal dash of bitters.
4. Mix gently.
5. Garnish with slice of lime.

CALORIES: 33

The unofficial Broadway Hall of Fame, Sardi's Restaurant, located in the heart of New York's theater district, has been a fixture there since 1921. It was current owner, Vincent Sardi's father who began it all with a character sketch in 1927 of a now-forgotten comic. Today, the walls are lined with drawings of actors, authors, and athletes. Sardi alone chooses those to be honored, the first qualification being that the person must have eaten at least once at the restaurant. Now it is up to Vincent Sardi to ensure that each celebrity is seated near his or her sketch.

By the way, the Casey Special is named in honor of a former classmate of Sardi who chose to quit drinking alcohol.

Opus One
Spiced Tonic

3 dashes Angostura
bitters
8 ounces tonic water
Several orange slices

1. Fill a large tumbler with ice.
2. Add 3 dashes of bitters.
3. Fill glass with tonic water.
4. Garnish with orange slices.

CALORIES: 88

The new Motown sounds are the rumblings of happy tummies. Chef Peter Loren smokes all his meats, poultry, and seafood, bakes the bread, whips up the sauces, and creates the desserts, all on site, for his American cuisine with a French flair. No wonder Opus One, in Detroit, has won so many honors: the city's 1993 restaurant of the year award, given by *Detroit Monthly* magazine; and two Five Star Diamond Awards in 1991, as one of the top fifty continental restaurants and as one of the top fifty restaurants in the United States.

Gerard's Place
McPherson

1 bunch mint
4 ounces lemon juice
2 tablespoons sugar
1 tablespoon grenadine
8 ounces orange juice
40 ounces tonic water
4 lemon slices

1. Chop the mint and marinate it with the lemon juice and sugar overnight in a mixing glass.
2. Add grenadine and orange juice, and mix thoroughly.
3. Pour into four highball glasses over ice.
4. Fill glasses with tonic water.
5. Garnish with a slice of lemon.
(Yield: 4 servings)

CALORIES: 184 per serving

The skills in chef/owner Gerard Pangaud's résumé—he formerly ran a two-star Michelin restaurant in Paris and later worked his magic at the Ritz-Carlton in Washington, D.C.—are put to good use at this seventy-seat, nonchalantly elegant restaurant near McPherson Square, two blocks from the White House. Gerard's Place was selected as one of *Esquire*'s best new restaurants of 1993 on the strength of such dishes as salad of salmon confit.

Pat O'Brien's
The Hurricane

4 ounces hurricane mix
2 ounces Collins mix
2 ounces water
1 orange slice and cherry
    as garnish

1. Fill a lantern-shaped glass or hurricane glass with shaved ice.
2. Pour in ingredients.
3. Mix well.
4. Garnish with orange slice and place a cherry on top of drink.

CALORIES: 290

One of New Orleans's favorite haunts, and famous for its Hurricanes, Pat O'Brien's Bar supplies a carnival atmosphere every night—not only during Mardi Gras. Spontaneity reigns in the piano bar, where even an Aunt Bertha from Omaha can be coaxed into singing for the crowd. Pat O'Brien also has a more sedate patio bar in a courtyard at the rear of the building, and a third bar by the entrance, favored by the locals.

Tony's
John Collins

1 ounce lemon juice
1 heaping teaspoon
    powdered sugar
6 ounces ginger ale
1 cherry
1 sprig mint

1. In a mixing glass, add lemon juice, sugar, and a splash of ginger ale.
2. Blend well.
3. Fill a tall or Collins glass with ice.
4. Strain mixture into glass.
5. Fill glass with ginger ale.
6. Garnish with a cherry and a sprig of mint.

CALORIES: 81

At Tony's on Market Street in St. Louis, guests indulge in house-made pastas, seafood, veal, and prime sirloin steak. The restaurant has won the Mobil Five Star Award for the past eighteen years, and the AAA Five Diamond Award for the past five. The cuisine may be surpassed only by the pampering each guest receives from the owner, Vincent J. Bommarito.

Hawk 'n' Dove
More Than a Shirley Temple

A good-sized splash of grenadine
7 ounces ginger ale
Your favorite fruit, such as orange slices or cherries

1. Fill a Collins glass with ice.
2. Add a good-sized splash of grenadine.
3. Pour in ginger ale.
4. Garnish with lots of fruit.

CALORIES: 97

Vanilla Coke

1 very short splash vanilla extract
12 ounces cola

1. Fill tumbler with ice.
2. Add a very short splash of vanilla extract.
3. Fill glass to the rim with cola.

CALORIES: 151

Cherry Coke

2 ounces grenadine
10 ounces cola
1 cherry

1. Fill a tumbler with ice.
2. Pour in grenadine and cola.
3. Garnish with a cherry.

CALORIES: 300

"A splash of vanilla goes a long way," says Sue Reid, manager of the Hawk 'n' Dove Restaurant in Washington, D.C. So she urges caution when mixing the Vanilla Coke. "It's from the soda fountain days. Our older patrons like it." Reid says the Hawk 'n' Dove is like a neighborhood saloon. Except the neighborhood is Capitol Hill, and the regulars are legislators and their staffs. Senator Bob Packwood was a regular, until his brush with the Ethics Committee.

The Rainbow Room
Spiked Cola

4 dashes Angostura
bitters
6 ounces cola
1 lemon wedge

1. Fill a highball glass with ice.
2. Add bitters.
3. Pour in cola.
4. Squeeze in lemon juice and add wedge.

CALORIES: 80

Lime Rickey

1 ounce lime juice
1 ounce simple syrup
3 dashes Angostura
bitters
6 ounces club soda
Spiral piece of lime peel

1. Fill Collins or iced-tea glass with ice.
2. Pour in lime juice, syrup, and bitters.
3. Top glass with club soda.
4. Garnish with a spiral piece of lime peel.

CALORIES: 100

Lemon Daisy

1 ounce grenadine
Juice of 1 lemon
1½ ounces 7-Up
1½ ounces club soda
Piece of lemon peel

1. In a white-wine glass, stir together the grenadine and lemon juice.
2. Add ice.
3. Top off glass with equal amounts of 7-Up and club soda.
4. Garnish with a lemon peel.

CALORIES: 110

High atop the Rockefeller Plaza, on the sixty-fifth floor of the GE Building, The Rainbow Room is *the* place for gazing at the Empire State Building and all of Manhattan. It's also *the* place for drinking, with its rich mahogany bar and delicious nonalcoholic cocktails, many of which are head bartender Dale DeGroff's own concoctions.

Fog City Diner

Lime Rickey

Juice of ½ lime
1 shot Rose's lime juice
1 shot sweet-and-sour
   mix
1 shot simple syrup
4 ounces ice
3 ounces club soda
3 ounces 7-Up or Sprite

1. Squeeze the juice from ½ lime into shaker cup.
2. Add next four ingredients.
3. Shake well.
4. Pour with ice into 16-ounce glass.
5. Add equal parts club soda and 7-Up or Sprite to fill.

CALORIES: 180

Fog City Lemonade

1½ ounces lemon juice
1½ ounces simple syrup
3 ounces ice
6 ounces club soda
1 lemon twist

1. Place first three ingredients in shaker cup.
2. Shake well.
3. Pour with ice into 12-ounce glass.
4. Add club soda to fill.
5. Garnish with a lemon twist.

CALORIES: 144

Although it specializes in classic diner fare, San Francisco's Fog City Diner also features inventive California cuisine. This means that a person who hankers for a chili dog and onion rings can share a table with someone who's addicted to Fog City's fabulous lobster chowder or the distinctive quesadilla with roasted hazelnuts.

Peer Inn
Lemon Limey

3 ounces margarita mix
6 ounces 7-Up
2 lime wedges

1. Fill a rocks glass with ice.
2. Add margarita mix.
3. Pour in 7-Up.
4. Squeeze a wedge of lime into drink.
5. Add lime wedge.
6. Mix well.

CALORIES: 187

San Francisco's Peer Inn, on Pier 33, is what Boston's Bull & Finch used to be before "Cheers" got ahold of it. The regulars, local San Franciscans who realize the bar has the best view of the San Francisco Bay and its shipping activities, have been patronizing the establishment for thirty-five years. Gina, the Peer Inn's only bartender, loves this drink for its "lemon limey taste." She compares it to "sparkling lemonade."

Gosman's
Pink Lemonade

2 ounces sour mix
3 ounces 7-Up
1 ounce cranberry juice
1 lemon slice

1. Mix first three ingredients in a mixing glass.
2. Pour into a 10-ounce Collins glass over ice.
3. Garnish with a generous slice of lemon.

CALORIES: 106

Situated at the entrance of Montauk Harbor, at the eastern tip of Long Island, Gosman's Restaurant and Bar is a perfect place to watch the summer pageant of yacht traffic. Gosman's location amid the saltwater breezes allows the restaurant to offer another sensual pleasure for diners: wonderfully fresh seafood, particularly lobster.

Nice Over Ice

Fruit Punches, Coolers,
and Spritzers

Karl Ratzsch's Old World Restaurant
Cardinal Punch

3 ounces orange juice
3 ounces cranberry juice
3 ounces ginger ale
3 to 4 ice cubes
1 orange slice
1 cherry

1. Pour first three ingredients into blender or shaker cup.
2. Blend well.
3. Pour over ice into tall rocks or Collins glass.
4. Garnish with skewered orange slice and cherry.

CALORIES: 142

Karl Ratzsch's Old World Restaurant in Milwaukee offers all of the amenities that attract people to a traditional German dining room: hearty helpings of tender sauerbraten, Wiener schnitzel, roast duckling and goose; antique beer steins and decorative plates on walls that rise to a large-beamed Alpine ceiling; and waitresses clad in peasant dresses known as dirndls. The Ratzsch family took a hands-on approach to running the restaurant when they opened it in 1904; they still do.

Mark's Place
Tropical Fruit Punch

2 ounces 7-Up or Sprite
4 ounces fresh-squeezed orange juice
4 ounces fresh-squeezed grapefruit juice
4 ounces cranberry juice
1 pineapple or orange slice
1 cherry

1. Pour 7-Up or Sprite over ice into 16-ounce glass.
2. Shake juices in shaker cup until foamy.
3. Add contents of shaker cup to the glass.
4. Stir.
5. Garnish with pineapple or orange slice and cherry.

CALORIES: 183

Southern Florida cuisine reaches its zenith in Miami at Mark's Place, where owner/chef Mark Militello emphasizes regional ingredients enhanced with Caribbean flavors. The fresh fish are plucked from nearby waters, most of the vegetables are locally grown, and venison and rabbit are farmed in state. Imported delicacies such as West Indian pumpkins or Jamaican yams add an exotic accent.

L'Orangerie
Framboise Fruit Punch

2 ounces orange juice
1 ounce sweetened passion fruit puree
1 ounce pineapple juice
4 ounces unsweetened raspberry (*framboise*) puree
1 orange slice
1 cherry

1. Pour the orange juice, sweetened passion fruit puree, and pineapple juice into a sour glass or Collins glass. If prefered, serve over ice.
2. Fill the rest of the glass with unsweetened raspberry (*framboise*) puree.
3. Garnish with skewered orange slice and cherry.

CALORIES: 112

"This makes a very unique tasting drink that is not heavy with sweetness, and leaves a very refreshing aftertaste," says Michael Simmons, bar manager of L.A.'s most renowned French restaurant. Whether it's lunch in the garden or dinner by candlelight in the dining room, Chef Jean-Claude Parachini's creations display a rare gift for using spices.

The Regent

Sportsman

1 ½ ounces orange juice
1 ½ ounces grapefruit
 juice
¼ ounce lemon juice
1 ounce cranberry juice
1 egg yolk
1 orange wedge
1 Amarena cherry
1 orchid

1. Fill a shaker cup with ice.
2. Pour first five ingredients into
 shaker cup.
3. Shake well.
4. Strain into a balloon glass.
5. Garnish with an orange wedge,
 Amarena cherry, and an orchid.

CALORIES: 429

Fruit Punch

2 ½ ounces orange juice
2 ½ ounces pineapple
 juice
2 ½ ounces 7-Up
½ ounce cranberry juice
¼ ounce grenadine
Pineapple wedge and
 orchid

1. Pour ingredients into a shaker cup
 filled with ice.
2. Shake.
3. Strain over ice into a balloon glass.
4. Garnish with a pineapple wedge and
 an orchid.

CALORIES: 127

Warren Beatty, Michael Eisner, the Prince of Wales, Princess Anne, Prince Andrew, Princess Margaret, King Hussein of Jordan, presidents Carter, Ford, and Reagan, King Olav of Norway, and the Dalai Lama. One of the most popular "rooms" at the luxury hotel, located on Wilshire and Rodeo, is the Presidential Suite. The six-room suite has been the palace-away-from-palace for Woolworth heiress Barbara Hutton, Elvis Presley, Ringo Starr, and singer Elton John, and has provided the set for Richard Gere and Julia Roberts in the film *Pretty Woman*. The price . . . $4,000 per night.

The Landing
Margarita

Salt
5 ounces sweet-and-sour
  mix
½ ounce Rose's lime juice
Wedge of lime

Straight up:
1. Salt the rim of a margarita glass.
2. Fill glass with ice. For frozen margarita, place sweet-and-sour mix and lime juice, plus two and a half ounces of ice, in a blender. Blend until a frozen mixture forms and pour into glass. Garnish with lime wedge.

On the rocks:
1. Pour in sweet-and-sour mix and lime juice.
2. Stir.
3. Garnish with lime wedge.

CALORIES: 140

Planter's Punch

5 ounces orange juice
5 ounces pineapple juice
1 ounce cranberry juice
1 splash grenadine
1 pineapple slice
1 orange slice
1 cherry

1. Place ⅛ cup of ice into a 12-ounce beer glass.
2. Pour ingredients into glass.
3. Stir.
4. Garnish with skewered pineapple and orange slices, and a cherry.

CALORIES: 183

A small Mexican restaurant at one end was the only establishment on San Antonio's River Walk when Jim Cullum opened the The Landing, thirty years ago, at the other end. "It was a brave thing to do, but an instant success," says Cullum. Built in the 1930s as part of a WPA project in the heart of the city, the walk along the San Antonio River was left unexploited for almost thirty years. Now second only to the

Alamo among the city's most popular attractions, the River Walk is filled with tempting fragrances from sidewalk cafes and the sounds of Mariachis. The Landing also boasts a seven-piece jazz band that performs every night except Sunday (when the band isn't busy recording another album or performing on National Public Radio). On Sunday a quintet takes over. Outside, on the terrace overlooking the river, a jazz duet performs during lunch.

Vincent Guerithault on Camelback
Vincent's Punch

2 ounces orange juice concentrate
½ ounce lemonade concentrate
1⅓ ounces cranberry juice
1⅓ ounces Hawaiian Punch
2 teaspoons sugar
2⅔ ounces water
¼ banana
1 heaping tablespoon fresh strawberries
3 scant tablespoons fresh rasperries
Sliced orange
Sliced lime
Sliced lemon

1. Combine first six ingredients in a highball glass.
2. In a blender, puree strawberries, banana, and raspberries with some of the punch mixture.
3. Blend fruit mixture until smooth, then add to punch.
4. Mix well.
5. If you prefer, strain punch through a fine sieve to remove any strawberry or raspberry seeds.
6. Chill well before serving.
7. Garnish with skewered orange, lemon, and lime slices.

CALORIES: 171

Escargot meets chilis. Perhaps no one except chef Vincent Guerithault could make classic French cuisine feel at home in the American Southwest—for example, consider the mesquite-grilled rack of lamb served with a spicy red and green pepper jelly and a smoking sprig of fresh rosemary, or the "duck tamale," which adds duck confit into a tamale made with corn masa and cilantro beurre blanc. Vincent's culinary talents and his Phoenix, Arizona, restaurant have won numerous awards. (Vincent's Punch recipe has been reduced from his party-size version.)

Fitzgerald's
Fruit Punch

4 ounces pineapple juice
4 ounces orange juice
1 squeeze lime
1 squeeze lemon
1 splash grenadine
1 orange slice
1 cherry

1. Pour first five ingredients into shaker cup.
2. Shake well.
3. Pour into a pint glass.
4. Garnish with skewered orange slice and cherry.

CALORIES: 150

Pineapple Soda

4 ounces pineapple juice
4 ounces club soda
1 splash orange juice
1 orange slice

1. Pour first two ingredients into shaker cup.
2. Shake well.
3. Pour into hurricane glass.
4. Add splash of orange juice.
5. Garnish with orange slice.

CALORIES: 76

Cranberry Soda

4 ounces cranberry juice
4 ounces club soda
1 squeeze lime
1 lime slice

1. Pour first two ingredients into shaker cup.
2. Shake well.
3. Pour into hurricane glass.
4. Top with squeeze of lime.
5. Garnish with slice of lime.

CALORIES: 73

In Houston, Texas, one of the best places to hear live music in a relaxing, down-home atmosphere is Fitzgerald's. On consecutive nights, bookings at the spacious nightclub might include a grunge band, a New

Age group, and the Neville Brothers. If the evening's headliner isn't music to your ears, head upstairs, where another act will soon take the stage.

The Boulders Resort
Passion Punch

3 ounces orange juice
3 ounces cranberry juice
1 ounce grapefruit juice
1 ounce pineapple juice
1 ounce sweet-and-sour mix
1 ounce Coco López cream of coconut
2 splashes grenadine
Cherry, orange, or pineapple for garnish

1. Fill 16-ounce plastic (for poolside drinking) glass with ice.
2. Add all ingredients except fruit and stir.
3. Garnish with skewered orange and pineapple pieces, or a cherry.

CALORIES: 300

The Boulders can refer to rocks or a resort. Found in Carefree, Arizona, both are unique in their own way. In the Sonoran Desert north of Phoenix, the rocks are a strange and special outcropping of granite boulders that are 12 million years old. The Boulders has been named one of the top twenty resorts on the mainland by *Condé Nast Traveler* and Andrew Harper's *Hideaway Report.* Built to reflect the sand and rocks of the desert, the resort complex features guest casitas, restaurants, and a main lodge—decorated with the colors and materials of the desert— as well as award-winning golf courses, pools, and tennis courts.

Blackwolf Run

Mandarin Punch

3 ounces orange juice
2 lemon wedges
4 ounces club soda
1 splash grenadine
1 pineapple piece

1. Fill a Collins glass with ice.
2. Add orange juice and the juice from the lemon wedges.
3. Fill glass with soda.
4. Lace with grenadine.
5. Garnish with pineapple.

CALORIES: 58

Cranberry Spritzer

3 ounces cranberry juice
½ ounce Rose's lime juice
4 ounces seltzer

1. Fill a Collins glass with ice.
2. Add juices.
3. Fill glass with seltzer.

CALORIES: 79

The bar at Blackwolf Run Golf Course in Kohler, Wisconsin, overlooks the Sheboygan River. If you prefer your water in a glass rather than in a hazard, the main dining room offers a panoramic view of the golf course. It also has a huge fieldstone fireplace and loft area, and for a feel of the outside indoors, there's a glass-walled dining porch. The view is of one of the two Pete Dye–designed championship 18-hole courses; this spectacular River course was named among the top four public courses in the nation by *Golf Digest*'s list of "America's 100 Greatest Golf Courses."

Snowbird Lodge Club
Pamela's Punch

2½ ounces fresh orange
juice
2½ ounces cranberry
juice
2½ ounces pineapple
juice
1 splash 7-Up (substitute
club soda or mineral
water to serve less
sweet)
1 lemon wedge

1. Fill a 16-ounce glass with ice.
2. Pour in juices and a splash of either
7-Up, club soda, or mineral water.
3. Garnish with lemon wedge and
serve with two bendable straws.

CALORIES: 117

Locals hang out in the Lodge Club bar at the Lodge in Snowbird, Utah,
relaxing in soft leather couches after a rough day on the slopes. The
Lodge Club's full-length windows allow visitors to marvel at Snowbird's
mountain, and make up lies about the runs they survived that day, such
as the 3½ mile run that drops 3,100 feet. The marble fireplace is perfect
for warm-ups, and the three-sided bar great for pick-me-ups or just pick
ups. Some customers argue that the bartenders, not the slopes, offer the
greatest danger. Twenty-five miles southeast of Salt Lake City in the
Little Cottonwood Canyon, Snowbird offers all the luxuries of the best
resorts.

The Tack Room
Punch

3 ounces orange juice
3 ounces pineapple juice
3 ounces sweet-and-sour
 mix
½ ounce grenadine
1 dash vanilla
1 fruit flag with pineapple
 spear

1. Fill a double old-fashioned glass with crushed ice.
2. In a mixing glass, blend all liquid ingredients.
3. Pour into the old-fashioned glass.
4. Garnish with flag and spear.

CALORIES: 201

Ten miles northeast of downtown Tucson, Arizona, the Vactor family has been hosting guests in their fifty-seven-year-old adobe hacienda since 1946. In 1993 it won the AAA Five Diamond Award, and it has won the Mobil Travel Guide Five Star Award for the past seventeen years. The Tack Room's old west hospitality extends to all its guests, including those who drink nonalcoholic cocktails. They may be enjoyed by the lounge fireplace, or in the dining room, which specializes in Southwestern cuisine.

John's Grill
Bloody Brigid

3 ounces fresh pineapple
 juice
1 ounce fresh lime juice
2 ounces sweet-and-sour
 mix
1 dash club soda
1 dash grenadine
½ teaspoon gum arabic
1 dash of a mixture of 7-
 Up and cherry juice
1 cherry for garnish

1. Fill a Collins glass filled with ice (unless you have a Maltese Falcon souvenir glass from the grill).
2. Add all ingredients except cherry.
3. Mix well.
4. Garnish with small black bird or, failing that, a cherry.

CALORIES: 132

(May substitute ¼ teaspoon sugar and ¼ teaspoon corn-starch for gum arabic)

"He (Sam Spade) went to John's Grill, asked the waiter to hurry his order of chops, baked potato, and sliced tomatoes . . ." Dashiell Hammett's Sam Spade, from *The Maltese Falcon*, ate and drank there, as people in San Francisco have been doing since 1908. The drink, of course, refers to Brigid O'Shaughnessy, Hammett's femme fatale, who was responsible for the death of Miles Archer, Spade's partner. The grill today celebrates the black bird with a Maltese Falcon Room, Hammett's Den, and mystery memorabilia.

The Rendezvous Lounge
Broadmoor Punch

1 ounce orange juice
1 ounce pineapple juice
1 ounce sweet-and-sour
   mix
1 ounce cranberry juice
7 ounces 7-Up
1 splash grenadine
1 candied fruit slice

1. Fill hurricane glass with ice.
2. Pour in juices.
3. Fill glass with 7-Up.
4. Top with a splash of grenadine.
5. Add fruit slice for garnish.

CALORIES: 202

The Broadmoor, a mountain resort with a view of Cheyenne Mountain and the city of Colorado Springs, encompasses 3,000 acres filled with suites, three championship golf courses, eight restaurants, and its own pharmacy and movie theater. Presidential guests have had a rightist bent, with Eisenhower, Nixon, Ford, Reagan, and Bush having stayed here. Entertainers Bob Hope, Jimmy Stewart, and John Wayne have sought solitude at the Mobil Five Star and AAA Five Diamond award-winning hotel. The Broadmoor offers six lounges, such as Spec's Spot, a sports bar; The Tavern Lounge, with piano music during the day and a four-piece orchestra at night; Penrose Lounge, with old-world English decor and the best views of Cheyenne Mountain and Colorado Springs; and The Rendezvous Lounge, a laid-back bar with quiet piano music and *the* spot for watching the lights dance on Cheyenne Lake.

Big Sky Café
Palace Punch

3 ounces orange juice
2 ounces pineapple juice
1 ounce grapefruit juice
½ ounce lime juice
½ ounce lemon juice
1 splash grenadine
Orange or lime slices, or cherry

1. Fill a 13-ounce chimney glass with ice.
2. Add all the juices.
3. Top with splash of grenadine.
4. Garnish with orange or lime slices, or cherry.

CALORIES: 100

Your grandma's favorite fried chicken recipe meets nouvelle cuisine. The Big Sky Café, in Webster Groves, Missouri, features "revitalized American favorites"—herb encrusted pork loin with Dijon pan gravy, roasted-garlic mashed potatoes, pecan encrusted catfish with fresh basil butter, and deep chocolate waffles with chocolate-chunk ice cream.

The Milton Inn
Orcranso Cooler

3 ounces orange juice
1 ounce cranberry juice
1 ounce pomegranate juice
Unflavored Seltzer
1 orange slice

1. Pour the orange, cranberry, and pomegranate juices into a shaker cup.
2. Shake well.
3. Fill a Collins glass with ice.
4. Pour mixture into the Collins glass.
5. Top off the cooler with unflavored Seltzer.
6. Garnish with orange slice.

CALORIES: 109

Gourmet magazine called the Milton Inn "the favorite haunt of the jodhpur set," and its kitchen "the best in the state." Near Baltimore in Sparks, Maryland, the Milton Inn resides in a 240-year-old fieldstone building. In years past, it has been a coachstop for Quakers, the Milton Academy, a school for boys named in honor of poet John Milton. One alumnus was John Wilkes Booth, President Abraham Lincoln's assassin. Since 1947, it has been an inn where fine dining and nonalcoholic beverages may be enjoyed in a candlelit dining room or on the open-air garden terrace.

Doug's Body Shop
Cranberry Cooler

2 ounces cranberry juice
½ ounce lime juice
10 ounces ginger ale

1. Fill a shaker cup or mixing glass with ice.
2. Add cranberry juice and lime juice.
3. Shake or mix.
4. Strain mixture into a tall glass.
5. Fill the glass with ginger ale.

CALORIES: 149

Auto aficionados will feel they have died and gone to car heaven. People who just enjoy eating good food in a joint with a fun atmosphere won't feel too bad either. At Doug's Body Shop, in Ferndale in the Detroit area, you may dine in a '52 Edsel, '58 Packard, '60 Chrysler, '64 T Bird, or a '65 Mercedes. Cars line the walls like booths, with tables inside the cars. Walls are filled with hub caps, road signs, and other auto memorabilia. Lunch in a T Bird, or have dinner in an Edsel. Shift into overdrive to dance to the driving beat of Top 40, jazz, rock, or R & B.

Pinehurst Resort
Quinine Cooler

1 ¼ ounces fresh orange juice
1 ¼ ounces cranberry juice
1 splash pineapple juice
1 teaspoon grenadine
4 ounces tonic water
1 orange slice
1 cherry

1. Fill a 10-ounce Collins glass with ice.
2. Pour all ingredients except tonic water into the Collins glass.
3. Mix.
4. Fill glass with tonic water.
5. Garnish with skewered orange slice and cherry.

CALORIES: 96

With its seven championship golf courses, Pinehurst Resort and Country Club is one of America's most famous golf havens. Nicknamed "The Queen of the South," the resort boasts 510 deluxe accommodations, more than 20 tennis courts, carriage rides, and a full marina. It's no wonder that *Bon Appétit* considers it one of the top resorts in the United States. Golfers and nongolfers alike relax in the Ryder Cup Lounge.

Piperade
Piperade Cooler

6 ounces Knudson's cranberry juice
2 ounces pineapple juice
1 ounce orange juice with pulp
1 ½ ounces 7-Up
1 orange slice

1. Place all ingredients except orange slice in a blender.
2. Add ¹⁄₁₆ cup of ice.
3. Blend at high speed for 20 seconds or until mixture becomes frothy.
4. Pour into a red wine glass.
5. Garnish with orange slice.

CALORIES: 117

Part of the decor at Cleveland's Piperade is a 1920s bank vault. But the true gems on the premises are the modern American dishes created by

Chef Ali Barker. Selected by *Bon Appétit* as "one of the hottest new restaurants," the restaurant features *piperade*, a combination of tomatoes, bell peppers, and onions, served with many of the entrées. Barker has incorporated his skills honed as the original chef at New York's Union Square Cafe.

Old Havana Docks Lounge
Caribbean Cooler

3 ounces orange juice
3 ounces cranberry juice
3 ounces piña colada mix
1 ounce sweet-and-sour mix
1 splash grenadine

1. Pour all ingredients into a mixing glass with ice.
2. Strain ingredients into a tall glass.

CALORIES: 311

Every sunset in Key West, Florida, is an event, where jugglers, singers, mimes, food vendors, and souvenir hawkers gather at Mallory Square. All applaud when the sun's last colorful rays cease to reflect on the water. A perfect place to avoid the mob but still enjoy the event is at the Havana Docks Lounge, at the Pier House. The lounge, an old William R. Porter docks shipping office, comes to life with music and dancing. Another great place to enjoy the Key West life-style and weather is outdoors at the Beach Club.

Haussner's
Pink Lemonade

1 ounce Sun-Ripe lemon juice
1 ounce grenadine
½ cup ice (preferably crushed)
10 ounces water
1 cherry
1 orange slice

1. Pour the first two ingredients into a mixing glass.
2. Fill to the line with crushed ice and water.
3. Shake well.
4. Pour into a 15-ounce squall glass.
5. Garnish with cherry and orange slice.

CALORIES: 107

Opened in 1926, Haussner's Restaurant in Baltimore, Maryland, boasts one of the nation's more impressive private nineteenth-century collections of etchings, china, sculptures, and paintings, including original works by Rembrandt and Gainsborough. Diners find just as much inspiration in the menu, which features more than 100 entrées, including sauerbraten, seafood, and wild game prepared in an old-world manner.

Vidalia

Rosemary Lemonade

2 ounces sugar
1 sprig fresh rosemary
3 ice cubes
½ lemon
1 ounce fresh lemon
 juice
8 ounces water
1 lemon wheel or fresh
 sprig of rosemary for
 garnish

1. Muddle sugar with rosemary.
2. Squeeze juice from lemon half into a large shaker cup with ice cubes.
3. Add the lemon half, additional lemon juice, water, and muddled rosemary mixture.
4. Shake well.
5. Remove lemon half.
6. Pour contents of shaker into large iced-tea or water glass.
7. Garnish with a lemon wheel or fresh sprig of rosemary.

CALORIES: 177

Vidalia, in Washington, D.C., suggests a country manor house, with folk art on the hand-sponged walls and cabinets stocked with bric-a-brac and antique plates. Chef/owner Jeffrey Buben celebrates Provincial American cooking with dishes that reflect the nation's diverse regional cuisines and indigenous ingredients: trout from the Shenandoah Valley, salmon from Maine, scallops from Massachusetts, Vidalia onions from Georgia, and herbs and berries from nearby Maryland and Virginia farms.

Jake's Famous Crawfish Restaurant

Lemonade

6 sugar cubes
1 small lemon
12 ounces water
6 ice cubes
1 lemon wheel

1. Drop sugar cubes into a pint glass.
2. Squeeze juice from fresh lemon into the glass.
3. Muddle sugar and juice.
4. Fill with ice and water.
5. Place stainless-steel shaker over pint glass and secure a tight seal. (A shaker cup can be used in steps 5, 6, and 7.)
6. Shake vigorously at least 8 times (a back-and-forth piston motion performed over one's shoulder).
7. Pour from shaker into pint glass.
8. Garnish with lemon wheel.

CALORIES: 52

Limeade

6 sugar cubes
1 small lime
6 ice cubes
12 ounces water
1 lime wheel

1. Drop sugar cubes into a pint glass.
2. Squeeze juice from fresh lime into the glass.
3. Muddle sugar and juice.
4. Fill with ice and water.
5. Place stainless-steel shaker over pint glass and secure a tight seal. (A shaker cup can be used in steps 5, 6, and 7.)
6. Shake vigorously at least 8 times (a back-and-forth piston motion performed over one's shoulder).
7. Pour from shaker into pint glass.
8. Garnish with lime wheel.

CALORIES: 60

In Portland, Oregon, Jake's Famous Crawfish has been serving fish-house specials with a flair since 1892. Diners can choose from more than thirty seafood entrées, and can order one of several types of oysters by specifying the Pacific Northwest bay where they were harvested. While the fish is fresh, the setting is a throwback: Waiters are garbed in white service coats, and the dining rooms are done in brass, wood, and stained glass. Jake's popular drinks are made without shortcuts or blenders. Bowls of fruit adorn the bar, and the staff cuts and squeezes fresh lemons, limes, or oranges for every citrus drink.

Key Largo
Pink Thang

1¼ ounces cranberry juice
1¼ ounces orange juice
1¼ ounces pineapple juice
1 splash club soda
1 cherry
1 orange wheel

1. Mix the three juices well.
2. Top with splash of club soda.
3. Pour over ice in a chimney glass.
4. Garnish with a cherry and an orange wheel.

CALORIES: 74

Largo Shake

3 ounces pineapple juice
½ ounce cream of coconut
2 ounces cream
1 orange wheel
1 maraschino cherry

1. Place first three ingredients in a shaker cup.
2. Shake well.
3. Pour over ice into a tall chimney glass.
4. Garnish with skewered orange wheel and maraschino cherry.

CALORIES: 311

Citrus Cooler

3 ounces orange juice
½ ounce sweet-and-sour
  mix
1 splash lime juice
1 splash orange Italian
  syrup
1 splash 7-Up
1 orange wheel
1 cherry

1. Mix the first two ingredients.
2. Top with the next three ingredients.
3. Pour over ice in a chimney glass.
4. Garnish with skewered orange
   wheel and cherry.

CALORIES: 91

Key Largo restaurant and nightclub is known for nightly performances by some of Portland, Oregon's best R & B, blues, and rock and roll bands, as well as occasional bookings of nationally known jazz acts. Caribbean decor updates Key Largo's setting in a landmark brick building in the city's Historic Old Town neighborhood.

Resto Des Amis

Limeonade

2 ounces fresh lime juice
2 ounces fresh lemon
  juice
1 ounce pineapple juice
2 ounces ginger ale
1 lime wheel

1. Pour first four ingredients into
   shaker cup.
2. Shake well.
3. Pour into ice-filled 12-ounce highball
   glass.
4. Garnish with lime wheel.

CALORIES: 54

As proof that the proverb that too many cooks spoil the consommé is sometimes wrong, acclaimed chefs Guenter Seeger of Atlanta's Ritz-Carlton Dining Room and Jean-Louis Palladin of Washington, D.C.'s Watergate Hotel joined forces to open Resto des Amis in Atlanta, Georgia. Result? The French bistro was voted best new restaurant by *Atlanta* magazine and one of the nation's best new restaurants by *Esquire*.

Town & Country Lounge

Raspberry Kiss

6 ounces Ocean Spray
  Cran-Raspberry Drink
1 ounce orange juice
¼ teaspoon lime juice
Approximately 3 ounces
  club soda

1. Fill a tall glass with ice.
2. Pour in Ocean Spray, orange juice, and lime juice.
3. Top with club soda.

CALORIES: 124

Pink Lady

6 ounces pink grapefruit
  juice
2 ounces club soda
2 lemon wedges
1 cherry for garnish

1. Fill a highball glass with ice.
2. Pour in grapefruit juice.
3. Top with club soda.
4. Squeeze in lemon juice of one wedge.
5. Garnish with lemon wedge and cherry.

CALORIES: 56

Sweet Tart

3 ounces orange juice
2 ounces grapefruit juice
1 ounce cranberry juice
1 dash grenadine
2 ounces club soda
1 lime slice

1. Fill a highball glass with ice.
2. Add juices.
3. Add grenadine.
4. Top with club soda.
5. Garnish with lime slice.

CALORIES: 77

The Stouffer Mayflower Hotel is one of Washington, D.C.'s oldest and most luxurious four-star and four-diamond hotels. Since opening its doors in 1925, it has been known for fine service and beauty. Presidents from Calvin Coolidge on have celebrated their inaugurations here. The Town & Country Lounge, located in the hotel's lobby, offers a warm and comfortable English pub atmosphere.

Sage's Sages
B-Girl Cocktail

7 ounces of fresh orange
juice
1 ounce of club soda

1. Fill a Collins glass with ice.
2. Pour in orange juice and club soda.
3. Mix.

CALORIES: 98

Sage's Sages, a casually elegant suburban Chicago restaurant, is noted for its generous steaks and fresh seafood, served by candlelight. A pianist provides entertainment at the bar, which is typically filled with well-dressed workers from nearby offices. Sage's Sages offers free nonalcoholic drinks to designated drivers.

Michel's
Pacific Passion

1 slice fresh papaya
1 slice fresh pineapple
3 ounces fresh-squeezed
orange juice
1 ounce sweet-and-sour
mix
½ ounce coconut syrup
1 dash grenadine
1 cherry
1 pineapple wedge
1 orange slice
1 orchid

1. Place first six ingredients in a
blender.
2. Blend until smooth.
3. Pour into a tall glass.
4. Garnish with skewered cherry,
pineapple wedge, and orange slice,
then float orchid on top.

CALORIES: 295

At no other venue in Honolulu, Hawaii, would dining alone seem more depressing than at Michel's. The French restaurant—with its sparkling chandeliers, fine china and crystal, and its views of the Waikiki skyline and the beach at Diamond Head—is ideal for couples in the mood to pitch woo. Michel's has been recognized as the island's most romantic restaurant by "Lifestyles of the Rich and Famous" for the past five years, and has won awards from *Travel Holiday* for twenty-nine consecutive years.

Daisy Buchanan's
Virgin Grape Crush

4 ounces cranberry juice
4 ounces sweet-and-sour mix
1 huge splash club soda

1. Fill a Collins glass with ice.
2. Pour in equal parts cranberry juice and sweet-and-sour mix.
3. Add a splash of club soda.
4. Stir well.

CALORIES: 164

Sex on the Beach

4 ounces orange juice
4 ounces cranberry juice

1. Fill a Collins glass with ice.
2. Pour in orange and cranberry juice.
3. Stir well.

CALORIES: 128

Once part of Boston's Charles River tidal flat, the area known as Back Bay was filled with dirt in the 1800s, and soon was filled with houses of Boston's elite. Such is the locale of the Daisy Buchanan bar, named after a character in F. Scott Fitzgerald's book *The Great Gatsby*. At the bar, players from the Boston Celtics, Bruins, or Red Sox may be found, along with a smattering of movie and music personalities. Larry Bird, Jim Rice, Scott Cooper, and Lenny Kravitz have passed through the bar's door, which was taken from the old city hall.

Restaurant at The Little Nell
Coconut Julius

4 ounces fresh-squeezed
orange juice
4 ounces canned
pineapple juice
½ ounce Coco López
cream of coconut
1 ounce half and half
6 ounces of ice cubes
1 very thin orange slice

1. Add first five ingredients to a shaker cup.
2. Shake until frothy.
3. Strain and serve in an up martini glass.
4. Garnish with a very thin orange slice (floated).

CALORIES: 213

Since its debut in 1989, the Restaurant at The Little Nell Hotel in Aspen, Colorado, has seen honors accumulate as swiftly as a Rocky Mountain snowfall. Executive chef George Mahaffey's innovations have been recognized with a DiRoNa award, and the opulent restaurant was ranked among the top ten by *Restaurants & Institutions* magazine.

Dixie Belle Saloon
Sitting Bull Firewater

4 ounces orange juice
4 ounces pineapple juice
1 dash grenadine
1 dash club soda
1 lemon wedge
1 stemmed cherry

1. Pour juices, grenadine, and club soda into a tall glass.
2. Add ice.
3. Stir.
4. Garnish with lemon wedge and cherry.

CALORIES: 129

When Madonna was still dreaming of a career in Michigan, Dolly Parton grabbed her career by the throat and shook it till it gave her what she wanted. Big breasts and big hair helped, but that alone certainly wouldn't have taken her as far as she's gone, nor for as long. She's a woman who deserves her own theme park. Or two. The Dixie Belle Saloon is part of the Dixie Stampede Dinner attraction, owned by Parton's Dollywood entertainment park, with locations in Pigeon Forge, Tennessee, and Myrtle Beach, South Carolina. Feast on down-home favorites such as roasted chicken, hickory-smoked ribs, corn on the cob, and Dixie bread, while watching cowboys and cowgirls provide a spectacular display of horsemanship.

Pricci

Virgin Madras

4 ounces cranberry juice
4 ounces orange juice
1 squeeze of lime

1. Fill a mixing glass or shaker cup with ice.
2. Add the juices.
3. Mix or shake well until ingredients blend completely.
4. Fill highball glass with ice.
5. Pour mixture in glass.
6. Garnish with squeeze of lime.

CALORIES: 124

For its winning combination of contemporary decor with old-world Italian flavors, Atlanta's Pricci restaurant was chosen by *Esquire* magazine as one of the best new restaurants of 1992. Since then bartenders have been kept even busier during the long wait for tables.

CBGB
Whiskeyless Sour

6 ounces lemon mix
1 teaspoon sugar
1 splash seltzer
2 orange wedges
2 lemon or lime wedges

1. Place lemon mix, sugar, and seltzer in a large glass.
2. Squeeze juice from one orange wedge and one lemon or lime wedge into the glass.
3. Garnish with wedges of orange and lime or lemon.
4. Avoid the practice of CBGB's staff, which is to eat all the orange wedges before they can be used in drinks.

CALORIES: 85

CBGB & OMFUG is the legendary, yet still grungy, New York rock and roll club that provided some of the earliest bookings for such bands as The Ramones, Blondie, Living Colour, Helmet, and Talking Heads, who immortalized the place in their tune "Life During Wartime." The bar's name is an acronym for Country, Blue Grass, Blues and Other Music For Uplifting Gormandizers. The cavelike club still hosts live music seven nights a week.

The New York Four Seasons
The Landmark

4 ounces cranberry juice
4 ounces grapefruit juice
4 ounces club soda

1. Pour well-chilled cranberry juice and grapefruit juice into a shaker cup.
2. Mix thoroughly.
3. Pour juices into a goblet.
4. Top off with club soda.

CALORIES: 108

Meandering through the space created by architectural giants Philip Johnson and Ludwig Mies van der Rohe, you may meet giants of a different sort: Bill Blass, the Kissingers, or the Trumps. As part of the Seagram Building, on Park Avenue in Manhattan, the restaurant changes its plants, flowers, and menus to complement the seasons, as they have since 1959 when the restaurant opened. The wood-paneled Grill Room is the place to be seen during lunch, while the Pool Room, with its white Carrara marble pool, is for serious evening diners. The Four Seasons is the first restaurant in Manhattan to be designated a New York City landmark, hence the drink's name.

Rattlesnake Club
Summerade

2 ounces orange juice
2 ounces grapefruit juice
2 ounces cranberry juice
2 ounces lemon juice
1 ounce grenadine

1. Combine all ingredients in a 12-ounce or larger container.
2. Blend well.
3. Fill a Zombie glass with crushed ice.
4. Pour mixture over the ice, and serve.

CALORIES: 129

When people talk about fine dining in the Detroit area, the name you're most likely to hear is that of Jimmy Schmidt, recipient of the James Beard Award for the Best Chef in the Midwest. Schmidt, with partner Michael Ilitch, of Little Caesar's fame, owns several other restaurants, including Tres Vite, Cocina del Sol, Buster's Bay, and Stelline.

Swann Lounge
Swann Spritzer

6 ounces fresh-mixed
   fruit juice
2 ounces club soda or
   seltzer

1. Make a fresh-mixed fruit juice with such possible combinations as strawberry, raspberry, and blackberry, or orange, pineapple, and banana.
2. Fill a 10-ounce highball glass with ice.
3. In the glass, combine juice and your choice of either soda or seltzer.

CALORIES: 78

The Swann Lounge and Cafe, and the Fountain Restaurant, at the Four Seasons Hotel, in Philadelphia, cater to those who choose not to imbibe alcohol by featuring a different nonalcoholic drink each day. This is in addition to the array of drinks available every day. The Swann Lounge and Cafe affords a view of the namesake of the restaurants, the Swann Memorial Fountain. Complementing the drinks is the award-winning menu of The Fountain Restaurant.

Spring Creek Resort
Teton Sunset

4 ounces orange juice
4 ounces cranberry juice
¼ ounce heavy cream
¼ ounce grenadine
1 splash club soda
1 fanned strawberry

1. Fill 12-ounce bulb glass with ice.
2. Pour in orange juice.
3. Add cranberry juice.
4. Pour in heavy cream.
5. Add grenadine.
6. Top off with a splash of soda.
7. Garnish glass with a fanned strawberry.

CALORIES: 171

Actor Harrison Ford and quarterback Joe Montana could tell you about the view at the Spring Creek Resort, nestled 700 feet above Wyoming's

Jackson Hole and opening up to the Grand Teton Mountain Range. Or about the food at the restaurant, The Granary, which serves wild game, seafood, pastas, and soups. The year-round resort is popular among entertainment and sports figures who enjoy The Granary Lounge, sleigh rides, cross-country skiing, ice skating, tennis courts, pool, and horseback riding.

Cafe Annie's
Juice Blend

3½ ounces fresh-
   squeezed orange juice
3 ounces fresh-squeezed
   lime juice
2 ounces cranberry juice
1 orange slice
1 cherry

1. Blend all ingredients in blender.
2. Serve (over ice, if desired) in a Collins glass.
3. Garnish with an orange and cherry flag.

CALORIES: 133

In Houston, Texas, Cafe Annie's Robert Del Grande continues to surprise his devotees with adventurous variations on Tex-Mex cuisine. Among the highlights: mussel soup laced with spicy chili and garnished with a dollop of apple butter on a mussel shell; a black bean terrine with goat cheese, served with salsa and corn relish; and cinnamon-roasted pheasant with a green chili vinaigrette.

The Inn and Links at Spanish Bay
Unfuzzy Navel

3 ounces orange juice
3 ounces peach nectar
1 teaspoon lemon juice
1 dash grenadine
1 orange slice

1. In a shaker cup filled with ice, combine all ingredients except orange slice.
2. Shake well.
3. Strain mixture into a wine glass.
4. Garnish with orange slice.

CALORIES: 359

The Inn and Links at Spanish Bay, in Pebble Beach, California, has been named the number-one mainland resort by the readers of *Condé Nast Traveler* magazine. The Lobby Lounge, which serves the Unfuzzy Navel and other nonalcoholic beverages, affords the perfect spot to cozy up to the roaring fireplace and watch the action on the golf course, or to gaze at the Pacific Ocean.

The Mansion on Turtle Creek
Flying Red Horse

½ green pepper
1 cup tomato juice
1 dash Tabasco sauce

1. Thinly slice green pepper.
2. Put all but one slice of green pepper in a blender.
3. Add tomato juice and Tabasco sauce to blender.
4. Blend on high speed.
5. Fill a well-chilled highball glass with ice.
6. Pour mixture into glass.
7. Garnish with green pepper.

CALORIES: 45

The Mansion on Turtle Creek is in an upscale area of Dallas. It was originally built in 1925 as a home for Sheppard King, who had made his money in cotton. This sixteenth-century Italian Renaissance-style structure was refurbished in the late seventies and a hotel tower was built adjacent to the original building. King's living room, library, and the 125-foot veranda are now spacious dining areas where patrons sup on Southwestern cuisine. A walled patio beyond the veranda is the perfect place for nonalcoholic drinks. The bar, with an Italian marble floor, inlaid wood ceiling, and gilded doors, was once the King family dining room.

The Green Room at the Hotel Dupont
Citrus Quench

½ ounce orange juice
½ ounce lemon juice
½ ounce pineapple juice
1 dash grenadine
6 ounces 7-Up
1 orange slice
1 cherry

1. Pour first three ingredients into a shaker cup.
2. Add dash of grenadine.
3. Shake well.
4. Pour into highball glass filled with ice cubes.
5. Add 7-Up to fill.
6. Garnish with skewered orange slice and cherry.

CALORIES: 118

In historic Wilmington, Delaware, the luxurious Hotel Du Pont is the jewel of the city's downtown. The place to dine at a leisurely pace is the hotel's Green Room, where the service is attentive, the Continental cuisine is first-rate, and the incredible Andrew Wyeth paintings on the walls are, in fact, originals.

Louie's Backyard
A'Justin

3 ounces orange juice
3 ounces pineapple juice
3 ounces Sprite
Splash fresh-squeezed
  key lime juice
1 orange slice
1 cherry

1. Pour first three ingredients into shaker cup.
2. Shake well.
3. Pour over ice into a Collins glass.
4. Add splash of key lime juice.
5. Top with skewered orange slice and cherry.

CALORIES: 127

Louie's Backyard, a cherished Key West haunt of Jimmy Buffet and Tom McGuane, is a registered national landmark. In the early 1900s, a shipwreck salvager used his profits to build a home with Doric columns and a two-story porch. Now, after a careful renovation and expansion, the structure includes outdoor dining decks that lead down to the ocean, and a kitchen that produces lavish Caribbean dishes. The A'Justin is named for the bartender who created it: Justin, a recovering—or adjusting—alcoholic.

Mother's
Fruit Juice Medley

2 ounces grapefruit juice
2 ounces pineapple juice
2 ounces orange juice
2 ounces cranberry juice
1 splash 7-Up

1. Fill a tall glass with ice.
2. Combine the four juices in the tall glass.
3. Stir briskly.
4. Add a splash of 7-Up.

CALORIES: 112

The Original Mother's Nightclub is one of the landmarks of Chicago's neon-dappled, booze-soaked Rush Street neighborhood. The bar has long been a mecca for tourists, college students, business people, and attractive members of both sexes who are looking to mate. Mother's provided the setting for the courtship of Rob Lowe and Demi Moore in *About Last Night . . .* , which was filmed on location.

The Rainbow Room
Virgin Royal Hawaiian

3 ounces pineapple juice
2 ounces orgeat (sweet, almond-flavored nonalcoholic syrup)
1 ounce lemon juice

1. Pour all ingredients into a shaker cup filled with ice.
2. Shake well.
3. Strain into a rocks glass.

CALORIES: 254

O.J. Tingles

5 ounces orange juice
3 dashes Angostura bitters

1. Fill a goblet with ice.
2. Add orange juice and bitters.
3. Stir.

CALORIES: 71

High atop the Rockefeller Plaza, on the sixty-fifth floor of the GE Building, The Rainbow Room is *the* place for gazing at the Empire State Building and all of Manhattan. It's also *the* place for drinking, with its rich mahogany bar and delicious nonalcoholic cocktails, many of which are head bartender Dale DeGroff's own concoctions.

Charley's Crab GR Steamer Bar
Margano Rita

2½ ounces Rose's lime juice
2½ ounces sweet-and-sour mix
½ ounce 7-Up
1 lime wheel

1. Pour all ingredients except lime into a spindle mixer in the order listed.
2. Blend until frothy.
3. Salt the rim of a margarita glass.
4. Pour ingredients into glass.
5. Garnish with a lime wheel.

CALORIES: 261

Charley's Crab, located in the heart of President Jerry Ford's hometown, is known throughout western Michigan for serving exceptionally fresh seafood. Overlooking the Grand River, in downtown Grand Rapids, Michigan, the restaurant and bar offer plenty of windows from which to watch the river meander by, and a patio for warm-weather service. Within the restaurant, the GR Steamer Bar serves up lighter fare—pastas and sandwiches—and live jazz nightly.

The Frog and the Redneck
Awesome Fresh Juices

3 ounces fresh-squeezed orange juice
3 ounces grapefruit juice
1 ounce cranberry juice
1 cup shaved ice
1 fresh lime slice
1 fresh orange slice

1. Pour all juices and 1 ounce of ice in shaker glass.
2. Shake.
3. Pour into tall glass filled with shaved ice.
4. Garnish with lime and orange slices.

CALORIES: 84

Richmond, Virginia, is the site of an unlikely alliance of chefs: Frenchman Jean-Louis Palladin (also of the Watergate Hotel and Resto des Amis), and Southerner Jimmy Sneed. The serendipitous result is The Frog and the Redneck, a fetching eatery where the menu changes daily, and every dish is freshly made and prepared to order. Specialties include seafood, rotisserie lamb, and crabmeat ravioli with seafood salad.

The Ivy Grill
Malibu Madras

3 ounces fresh-squeezed
   orange juice
3 ounces pink grapefruit
   juice
3 ounces cranberry juice
3 ounces pineapple juice
Splash of Coco López
   cream of coconut
1 orange slice
1 cherry

1. Pour first five ingredients over 3 or 4 ice cubes in poco grande glass.
2. Shake well.
3. Garnish with an orange and cherry flag.

CALORIES: 201

Now owned by Dartmouth College, The Hanover Inn is New Hampshire's oldest hotel. Students, faculty, alumni, and locals frequent its Ivy Grill for contemporary American cuisine in an Art Deco setting, or, in warm weather, on the terrace. For more elaborate fare in a formal atmosphere, they dine at the inn's Daniel Webster Room.

Sanford
Virgin Piña Colada

1 scoop ice
5 ounces pineapple juice
Juice of ½ lime
2 tablespoons Coco
   López cream of
   coconut
Dash simple syrup
1 pineapple wedge

1. Fill shaker cup with ice.
2. Add next four ingredients.
3. Shake until mixture is frothy, but not slushy.
4. Strain into an up glass.
5. Garnish with fresh pineapple wedge.

CALORIES: 240

The husband-and-wife team of Sanford and Angie D'Amato run Sanford, a fifty-seat, sixteen-table storefront restaurant in downtown Milwaukee. The French–New American menu, revised daily, is derived from French cooking, but draws on global influences. One example: an irresistible grilled red snapper on crab hash with red onion and pancetta vinaigrette.

Planet Hollywood
Pretty in Pink

2 ounces orange juice
2 ounces pineapple juice
2 ounces cranberry juice
¼ ounce Coco López
   cream of coconut
¼ ounce grenadine
Dash Rose's lime juice
1 orange slice
1 lemon slice
1 lime slice
1 cherry

1. Pour first six ingredients into shaker cup in order listed.
2. Shake well.
3. Pour over ice into a Collins glass.
4. Garnish with skewered slices of orange, lemon, and lime, and a cherry.

CALORIES: 160

Planet Hollywood restaurants cater to the famous and the famished in New York, Chicago, Aspen, Minneapolis, Costa Mesa, Washington, D.C., and elsewhere. Co-owners Bruce Willis, Sylvester Stallone, and Arnold Schwarzenegger donated some of the many movie props and costumes that lure the star-struck. Smoked chicken pizza, focaccia, pastas, and desserts—such as a brownie with ice cream immersed in hot fudge and caramel sauces—coax browsing diners back to their tables.

Bright Angel Lodge
El Tovar Delight

3 ounces pineapple juice
3 ounces orange juice
2 ounces cream
1 ounce Coco López
 cream of coconut
1 orange slice
1 cherry

1. Pour first four ingredients into blender.
2. Blend well.
3. Pour into a tulip glass.
4. Garnish with skewered orange slice and cherry.

CALORIES: 325

Situated on the South Rim of the Grand Canyon, the Bright Angel Lodge offers Southwestern dishes in its restaurant, and rustic but comfortable accommodations for sightseers and hikers in its cabins and main lodge. Window tables at one end of the restaurant feature marvelous views of the canyon's natural wonders; elsewhere in the room, stone fireplaces set a homey mood.

Kingston Mines
Easy Living

2 ounces orange juice
2 ounces pineapple juice
2 ounces cranberry juice
2 ounces 7-Up or Sprite
1 orange slice
1 cherry

1. Pour first four ingredients into blender.
2. Blend well.
3. Pour over ice into a Collins glass.
4. Garnish with skewered orange slice and cherry.

CALORIES: 134

For more than a quarter-century, the Kingston Mines has been the place for rockers such as Eric Clapton and Keith Richards to unwind after concerts in Chicago. Two stages in adjacent rooms offer alternating live blues bands; the late closing time (4 A.M. weeknights, 5 A.M. weekends) and accessibility from Lake Shore Drive make it a convenient place for musicians to drop in when they're in the mood to join an impromptu jam session.

Club Med Sandpiper
Chantaco

6 ounces fresh-squeezed
orange juice
1 ounce fresh-squeezed
lemon juice
1 splash grenadine for
color
1 orange slice
1 cherry

1. Fill tall glass with ice.
2. Add ingredients.
3. Allow grenadine to settle to the
bottom of the glass. (Drink may also
be served with ingredients mixed.)
4. Garnish with umbrella skewer of
orange slice and cherry.

CALORIES: 88

Notorious in the seventies and eighties for its nude beaches and wild
singles nightlife, Club Med has moved into the nineties with daycare
service and special activities for parents and children. With more than
fifteen villages around the world, Club Med offers upscale vacations as
the "antidote for civilization." Located in St. Lucie, Florida, north of
Palm Beach, the Club Med Sandpiper village encompasses 500 acres with
five pools, restaurants, a cocktail lounge, theater, and a disco, and
activities such as golf, tennis, scuba diving, sailing, and circus workshops.

The Tonga Room
Tonga Twist

3 ounces pineapple juice
3 ounces grapefruit juice
½ ounce grenadine
Club soda
1 pineapple wedge
1 cherry
1 sprig mint

1. Fill a tall glass with ice cubes.
2. Add pineapple and grapefruit juices,
and grenadine.
3. Stir.
4. Fill glass to the top with club soda.
5. Garnish with skewered pineapple
wedge and cherry, and a sprig of
mint.

CALORIES: 97

Built in 1907, San Francisco's historic Fairmont Hotel and its Tonga
Room have served ten United States presidents, world leaders, and

countless royalty. The Garden Room of the Fairmont hosted dignitaries as they drafted the charter for the United Nations. On a less grand, but more popular scale, the Fairmont provided the setting for the television series "Hotel."

Algonquin Hotel
The Blue Bar's Designated Cocktail

2 ounces unsweetened blueberry juice
½ ounce lime juice
¼ teaspoon bar (very fine) sugar

1. Place all ingredients in a mixer cup or closed container.
2. Stir. Add more sugar if necessary, to taste.
3. Fill an old-fashioned glass with ice.
4. Pour mixture into glass.

CALORIES: 171

Since 1902, The Algonquin has played host to literary and theatrical luminaries from around the world. New York's Algonquin, and its Blue Bar, provided the venue for the famed Algonquin Round Table, where Dorothy Parker, Robert Benchley, Alexander Woollcott, George S. Kaufman, Robert E. Sherwood, Heywood Broun, and others, set the style for young writers, and their wisecracks and opinions became the last word in twenties humor, and beyond. Other writers who have made the grande dame their home are William Faulkner, Sinclair Lewis, and Maya Angelou. The lobby, the most popular meeting place, ignores the trendy and instead offers comfortable sophistication.

Antone's
The Juicer

3 ounces pineapple juice
3 ounces cranberry juice
3 ounces orange juice

1. Fill Collins glass with ice.
2. Pour all 3 juices into the Collins glass.
3. Mix well.

CALORIES: 141

Antone's, in Austin, Texas, is nationally known as a premier rhythm-and-blues club. Big blues names such as Muddy Waters and B. B. King have frequented the club. And the music is king at this no-frills bar. It may look like your feet will stick to the floor, but they won't be stuck long. The music will get your feet tapping, and finally you won't be able to fight it any longer and you'll find yourself on the dance floor.

Waterway Cafe
Candy Apple Fizz

4 ounces cranberry juice
4 ounces apple juice
1 splash club soda
1 lime slice

1. Fill a Collins glass with ice.
2. Add equal parts of the juices.
3. Pour in splash of club soda.
4. Garnish with a slice of lime.

CALORIES: 108

Palm Beach, Florida, may be pretentious, but the Waterway Cafe in Palm Beach Gardens isn't. On the waterfront, surrounded by tropical scenery, diners delight in the fresh seafood and friendly service at the open-air restaurant. It's a favorite with locals.

And on Sundays and Wednesdays the Cafe cranks up the reggae music. People dance across a bridge to a floating bar, decorated with life preservers, to order their favorite nonalcoholic drink.

Buckhead Diner
Pellegrino Sunrise

1 small bottle (four ounces) San Pellegrino
2 ounces orange juice
2 ounces unflavored sparkling water
Lemon, orange, and lime slices

1. Fill Collins glass or frozen-drink glass with crushed or cubed ice.
2. Pour Pellegrino into glass.
3. Add orange juice and water.
4. To preserve tequila sunrise effect, don't stir.
5. Garnish with skewered lemon, orange, and lime slices.

CALORIES: 78

At Atlanta's Buckhead Diner, savvy eaters and celebrities such as Elizabeth Taylor, Elton John, and Stevie Wonder partake of grit cakes (a mixture of grits, collard greens, red-eye gravy, with diced tomato and onions), veal meatloaf and celery mashed potatoes, and desserts such as white-chocolate banana cream pie. The dishes are served in an opulent setting of exotic woods and delicate lighting—the atmosphere of an Orient Express railcar.

Stars
Virgin Royale

¾ ounce Monin nonalcoholic cassis
6 ounces Duché de Longueville nonalcoholic sparkling apple cider from Normandy (may substitute another French sparkling apple cider)
Lemon zest ·

1. Pour the cassis into a champagne flute.
2. Fill with apple cider.
3. Garnish with Lemon zest.

CALORIES: 143

Stars, Jeremiah Tower's gastronomic wonderland in San Francisco, serves contemporary American cuisine in an enormous dining room that is dominated by the city's longest bar. The local and visiting celebs who vie for tables are rewarded with selections from a menu that changes daily. The nonalcoholic cider from Normandy, served solo or as part of the Virgin Royale, is a very popular accompaniment to most dishes.

The Inn at Little Washington

Virginia Sunset

4 ounces Virginia
  sparkling cider
1 ounce pineapple juice
1 ounce cranberry juice
4 ice cubes
1 splash grenadine
1 orange slice
1 raspberry

1. Combine first three ingredients with 2 ice cubes.
2. Stir.
3. Strain into a white-wine glass over remaining ice.
4. Add a splash of grenadine to top.
5. Garnish with orange slice and raspberry.

CALORIES: 133

Pretty soon the drowsy town of Washington, Virginia, will need to install its first stoplight to slow the traffic speeding toward The Inn at Little Washington. Only The Inn glitters with *all* of the most coveted awards: five stars from the Mobil Travel Guide, five diamonds from AAA, the DiRoNa award, Restaurant of the Year honors from the James Beard Foundation for 1993, and . . . well, you get the idea. Getting a reservation is another matter: The Inn's twelve rooms are booked a year in advance.

Frozen Delights

Daiquiris, Coladas, Bellinis,
and Fruit Slushes

The '21' Club
Virgin Strawberry

1 ounce lemon juice
1 ounce fresh-squeezed
   orange juice
1 small dish strawberries
Sugar to taste
Ice to fill a stemmed glass
1 dash grenadine

1. Place all ingredients including ice in blender and blend well.
2. Pour into a stemmed glass.

CALORIES: 121

The '21' Club, long a magnet for Manhattan's publishing, entertaining, and business leaders, is noted for such menu items as Chicken Hash and the '21' Hamburger. The wood-paneled clubby barroom is adorned with such memorabilia as model-size company trucks, to commemorate the executives who have bent an elbow in the bar during its six decades. Formal dining rooms are up the stairs.

Strings
Slush

4 ounces orange juice
4 ounces frozen
   strawberries
1 fresh banana
3–4 ice cubes
1 fresh strawberry

1. Place first four ingredients in blender.
2. Blend until texture is slushy.
3. Pour into a large tulip glass.
4. Garnish with a fresh strawberry.

CALORIES: 225

When the national touring companies for such theatrical extravaganzas as *Phantom of the Opera* and *Cats* descend on Denver, Colorado, the cast parties invariably are staged at Strings. The casual-contemporary cuisine, heavily influenced by the chef's seafood salad days in California, soothes entertainers homesick for Spago.

The Grand Cafe
Red Passion

1 cup chopped
strawberries
6 ounces fresh-squeezed
orange juice
½ cup diced papaya
2 whole strawberries

1. Place first three ingredients in a blender.
2. Blend until smooth.
3. Pass mixture through a strainer.
4. Chill, covered, for at least 4 hours.
5. Stir well before serving, then pour into 2 highball glasses.
6. Garnish each drink with a fresh strawberry.

CALORIES: 82

Hailed recently by *Gourmet* as "the most accomplished chef in Miami" and "a master in top form," the Grand Cafe's Katsuo Sugiura is too focused to let the attention go to his head. Instead, he's busy crafting such delicate dishes as lamb loin smoked over oolong tea and hickory chips. The cafe, located in Coconut Grove's Grand Bay Hotel, features a light, airy decor embellished with exotic floral displays. The Sunday brunch is the best in town.

Tony's
Frozen Strawberry Daiquiri

4 ripe strawberries
2 teaspoons powdered
sugar
1 cup crushed ice
1 ounce fresh lemon
juice
1 strawberry and sprig of
mint

1. Place first four ingredients in a blender.
2. Blend until mixture is snowlike in texture.
3. Pour into a wine glass.
4. Garnish with a large ripe strawberry and a sprig of mint.

CALORIES: 62

At Tony's on Market Street in St. Louis, guests indulge in house-made pastas, seafood, veal, and prime sirloin steak. Tony's has been awarded the Mobil Five Star Award for the past eighteen years, and the AAA Five Diamond Award for the past five. The Italian cuisine is surpassed only by the pampering each guest receives from owner Vincent J. Bommarito.

Wish's
Strawberry Daiquiri

2 large strawberries
6 ounces sour mix
1 ounce sugar
4 ice cubes

1. Place all ingredients in a blender and blend until the ice is crushed.
2. Serve in a daiquiri glass.

CALORIES: 150

Wish's restaurant and pub provides a comfortable postgame hangout for players from the Chicago Bears, Blackhawks, and Cubs, as well as actors passing through Chicago, and neighborhood barflies. When the Cubs are in town, first baseman Mark Grace and actor Jim Belushi, co-owners of the pub, can sometimes be found huddled in front of a ball game on the big-screen TV, or leaning against a wall decked with black-and-white photos of celebrities.

Westin Resort
The Energizer

4 fresh strawberries
3 ounces Gatorade (any flavor, but the Resort staff prefers lime)
1 cup ice
1 tablespoon honey
½ banana
1 extra strawberry
Whipped cream

1. Place all ingredients except the extra strawberry and whipped cream in a blender.
2. Blend until frozen.
3. Pour into a hurricane glass.
4. Garnish with fresh strawberry and a small squeeze of whipped cream.

CALORIES: 151

The Westin Resort on Hilton Head Island, South Carolina, features a high-energy drink because guests need extra zip when they play on any of the three PGA championship golf courses, or the sixteen tennis courts, which offer all three types of Grand Slam playing surfaces.

The Painted Table, Alexis Hotel
Painted Lady

3 tablespoons frozen raspberries in syrup
½ cup ice
3 ounces water
1 splash grenadine
1 splash lemon sweet and sour `
1 ounce orange juice
⅛ cup ice
1 ounce water
1 splash lemon sweet and sour
1 cherry

1. Blend first five ingredients. (To make lemon sweet and sour, follow the directions on a package of Neilsons frozen lemon base, mixing lemon base with simple syrup in order to create the lemon sweet and sour.)
2. Pour mixture into a wine glass, filling it ¾ full.
3. Blend 1 ounce orange juice, ⅛ cup ice, 1 ounce water, and 1 splash lemon sweet and sour.
4. Fill wine glass with second mixture.
5. Garnish with cherry.

CALORIES: 94

The Alexis Hotel, located one block from Seattle's financial district, between trendy Pike Place Market and historic Pioneer Square, is an intimate fifty-four-room hotel offering three bars that serve nonalcoholic drinks. One of these bars, The Painted Table, has been honored by *Bon Appétit* as "one of Seattle's best places to spend the evening."

Mai-Kai

Tahitian Paradise

4 to 6 fresh strawberries
2 ounces milk or skim milk
1 ounce Coco López cream of coconut
1 ounce orange juice
1 ounce pineapple juice
3 to 4 ounces (about ½ cup) crushed ice
Mint leaves
1 additional strawberry

1. Place all ingredients except mint and one strawberry in a blender.
2. Blend for 10 to 15 seconds, adding crushed ice for the last few seconds. It is not meant to be a frozen drink so do not blend longer.
3. Pour drink into a 12- to 16-ounce tumbler.
4. Garnish with fresh mint leaves and strawberry. For an added touch, powder the mint leaves with sugar.

CALORIES: 161

Waikiki

1 ounce pineapple juice
1 ounce guava nectar
1 ounce papaya nectar
½ teaspoon honey, to taste
¼ cup crushed ice
1 slice kiwi or pineapple

1. Place first four ingredients in a blender.
2. Blend for 5 to 10 seconds, adding ¼ cup crushed ice for the last few seconds. Don't overblend. This is not meant to be a frozen drink.
3. Pour into a 6- to 8-ounce glass.
4. Garnish with a slice of kiwi or pineapple.

CALORIES: 63

King Kong would feel at home. The wind whispering through the large green leaves. The whooshing of waterfalls. The sway of native dancers. Oriental and Pacific Rim dishes. Tons of tourists and locals have visited since 1956, when Fort Lauderdale's Mai-Kai opened. The landmark Polynesian restaurant has Florida's longest-running night club floor show, the Island Revue—dancers perform two forty-five-minute shows nightly. Dress code: Grass skirt not required.

The Lodge at Pebble Beach
Johnny Miller Special

Ice to fill ⅓ blender
6 strawberries (or other
  seasonal berries)
1 banana
1 ounce orange juice
1 ounce pineapple juice
1 ounce apple juice (or
  cranberry juice if
  preferred)
1 sprig mint

1. Fill blender ⅓ full of ice.
2. Add all ingredients except for mint.
3. Blend to a smooth consistency.
4. Pour into a 12-ounce highball glass.
5. Garnish with sprig of mint.

CALORIES: 163

Pebble Beach offers some of the most beautiful and picturesque coastline vistas in California. It also has one of the world's most famous golf courses. Johnny Miller, the namesake of the drink, was a successful golfer at Pebble Beach in the mid-seventies. The Tap Room, at The Lodge, has a publike atmosphere, and is filled and decorated with a collection of championship golf memorabilia from the Crosby and AT&T Pro-Ams, and three U.S. Open championships.

Red Lion Inn
Toothless Red Lion

2 ounces sliced
  strawberries and juice
½ banana
½ ounce Rose's lime juice
4 ounces crushed ice
Cream to blend
1 sugared strawberry half

1. Combine first four ingredients in blender.
2. Add cream while blending until it blends smoothly.
3. Pour into a hurricane glass.
4. Garnish with a sugared strawberry half.

CALORIES: 188

A refurbished, old-fashioned country inn in the Berkshires, The Red Lion is as American as a Norman Rockwell painting—which is no coincidence.

Rockwell lived within a short stroll of the Red Lion in Stockbridge, Massachusetts, and painted many of the townsfolk and the inn itself for his popular magazine covers and illustrations. The artist was also one of the many regulars who enjoy several meals each week at the inn's homey dining room.

Kabby's Sports Edition
Strawberry Daiquiri

4 ounces strawberry
   daiquiri mix
1 dash simple syrup
4 ice cubes
1 Louisiana strawberry

1. Pour all ingredients except for the strawberry into blender.
2. Blend well.
3. Pour into a grande bowler.
4. Top with strawberry.

CALORIES: 224

Piña Colada

4 ounces piña colada mix
1 dash simple syrup
4 ice cubes
Orange slice
Whipped cream if
   desired

1. Pour all ingredients except for the orange slice and whipped cream into a blender.
2. Blend well.
3. Pour into a grande bowler.
4. Top with orange slice and, if desired, whipped cream.

CALORIES: 255

Kabby's Sports Edition at the New Orleans Hilton Riverside features twenty-nine television sets so your favorite basketball, football, baseball, or hockey team is never far away. Kabby's Seafood restaurant, adjacent to the sports bar, specializes in New Orleans favorites such as chicken and sausage gumbo, shrimp or oyster Po-Boys, or the classic Cajun combo of Jambalaya, red beans, and rice, with smoked sausage. With its 275-foot-long spread of windows, the restaurant provides views of the endless parade of traffic on the Mississippi River.

The Rendezvous Lounge
Virgin Strawberry Daiquiri

4 ounces sweetened
strawberries (frozen)
with juice
1 ounce sweet-and-sour
mix
1 dash grenadine
4 ice cubes
Whipped cream

1. Pour all ingredients except whipped cream into a blender with ice.
2. Blend until smooth.
3. Pour into a red-wine glass.
4. Garnish with whipped cream.

CALORIES: 142

Virgin Piña Colada

1 15-ounce can Coco
López cream of
coconut
3 6-ounce cans pineapple
juice
4 ice cubes
1 orange slice
Cherry

1. Mix cream of coconut and pineapple juice to make a piña colada mix.
2. Pour 5 ounces of the mix into a blender with ice.
3. Blend until smooth.
4. Pour into a red-wine glass.
5. Garnish with orange slice and cherry.

CALORIES: 311

The Broadmoor, a mountain resort with a view of Cheyenne Mountain and the city of Colorado Springs, Colorado, has 3,000 acres filled with suites, three championship golf courses, eight restaurants, and its own pharmacy and movie theater. Presidential guests have had a rightist bent, with Eisenhower, Nixon, Ford, Reagan, and Bush having stayed here. Entertainers Bob Hope, Jimmy Stewart, and John Wayne have sought solitude at the Mobil Five Star and AAA Five Diamond award-winning hotel. The Broadmoor offers six lounges, such as Spec's Spot, a sports bar; The Tavern Lounge, with piano music during the day and a four-piece orchestra at night; Penrose Lounge, with old-world English decor and the best views of Cheyenne Mountain and Colorado Springs; and The Rendezvous Lounge, a laid-back bar with quiet piano music and *the* spot for watching the lights dance on Cheyenne Lake.

Disneyland Hotel
Virgin Frozen Strawberry Colada

2 ounces Island Oasis
   strawberry mixer
4 ounces piña colada
   mixer
6 ounces ice
Dollop of whipped
   cream
1 strawberry

1. Place first three ingredients in
   blender.
2. Blend to desired thickness.
3. Pour into a 12-ounce glass.
4. Top with dollop of whipped cream
   and a strawberry.

CALORIES: 314

Strawberry-Banana Margarita

3 ounces Island Oasis
   strawberry mixer
3 ounces Island Oasis
   banana mixer
2 ounces margarita or
   sweet-and-sour mix
4 ounces ice

1. Place all ingredients in blender.
2. Blend to desired thickness.
3. Pour into 12-ounce glass.

CALORIES: 193

Opened in 1955 as a family resort linked by monorail to Disney's Magic Kingdom in Anaheim, California, the Disneyland Hotel is anything but a Mickey Mouse operation. With 1,131 rooms in three towers and garden villas, plus three swimming pools, ten tennis courts, and a fitness center, the hotel hosts business conventions as well as tourists. Guests can choose from eleven theme restaurants and lounges, including the Neon Cactus country-western saloon.

Juanita's
Virgin Strawberry Daiquiri

½ cup fresh strawberries
2 ounces sweet-and-sour mix
1 scoop ice
6 tablespoons whipped cream
1 orange slice
1 cherry

1. Place first three ingredients in blender.
2. Add one squirt (about 4 tablespoons) whipped cream to blender.
3. Blend until frothy.
4. Pour into a 16-ounce soda glass.
5. Garnish with an orange/cherry flag.
6. Top with a swirl (2 tablespoons) of whipped cream.

CALORIES: 134

Virgin Piña Colada

½ cup Coco López cream of coconut
1¼ ounces pineapple juice
1¼ ounces sweet-and-sour mix
1 scoop ice
1 orange slice
1 cherry

1. Place first four ingredients in blender.
2. Blend until frothy.
3. Pour into a 16-ounce soda glass.
4. Garnish with an orange/cherry flag.

CALORIES: 464

Juanita's Restaurant would qualify as a Little Rock landmark solely on the basis of its exceptional Tex-Mex platters made with fresh ingredients and homemade tortillas, fashioned into spinach enchiladas, beef enchiladas, tamales, and chicken tacos. The fact that its bar, in the room next door, offers the area's best live music—from unplugged guitarists to high-decibel hard rockers to zydeco washboard strummers—is a pleasant bonus.

Planet Hollywood
Home Alone

½ banana
2 ounces fresh
strawberries
3 ounces piña colada mix
Splash grenadine
1 scoop ice
1 strawberry

1. Place first five ingredients in blender and blend well.
2. Pour into a Collins glass.
3. Garnish with a strawberry.

CALORIES: 250

Planet Hollywood restaurants cater to the famous and the famished in New York, Chicago, Aspen, Minneapolis, Costa Mesa, Washington, D.C., and elsewhere. Co-owners Bruce Willis, Sylvester Stallone, and Arnold Schwarzenegger donated some of the many movie props and costumes that lure the star-struck. Smoked chicken pizza, focaccia, pastas, and desserts—such as a brownie with ice cream immersed in hot fudge and caramel sauces—coax browsing diners back to their tables. The Home Alone is the restaurants' most popular drink.

Biba Restaurant
Blushing Bellini

¼ fresh peach, skinned
and pitted
2 ounces peach nectar
2 ounces club soda
4 ounces ice
4 fresh raspberries

1. Place first four ingredients in blender.
2. Blend until frothy.
3. Serve in champagne flute.
4. Garnish with fresh raspberries.

CALORIES: 82

In Boston, the place to go if one wishes to be overwhelmed is Biba. With Lydia Shire at the helm, this restaurant gives diners a dual opportunity: to gaze out at the Public Garden, the oldest botanical garden in America; and to enjoy such culinary epiphanies as the one described on the menu as, "Marsala mousse melting in hot chocolate soup with almond macaroons."

Cafe Annie's
Virgin Bellini

1 whole fresh peach
4 ounces lime juice
4 ounces club soda
4 ounces ice cubes

1. Slice peach into sections, removing stem, skin, and pit. Reserve one slice for garnish.
2. Place all ingredients except the peach slice in blender.
3. Blend to desired consistency.
4. Pour into a wine glass.
5. Garnish with peach slice.

CALORIES: 74

In Houston, Texas, Cafe Annie's Robert Del Grande continues to surprise his devotees with adventurous variations on Tex-Mex cuisine. Among the highlights: mussel soup laced with spicy chili and garnished with a dollop of apple butter on a mussel shell; a black bean terrine with goat cheese, served with salsa and corn relish; and cinnamon-roasted pheasant with a green chili vinaigrette.

Tony's
Nonalcoholic Bellini

4 medium-sized peaches
2 teaspoons powdered
   sugar
Juice of 2 lemons
1 bottle Martinelli's
   Sparkling Cider (750
   ml)

1. Peel and pit peaches.
2. Place the peaches in a blender and puree them completely.
3. Transfer the contents of the blender into a pitcher.
4. Slowly pour the bottle of sparkling cider over the peaches, then gently stir the two together.
5. Pour into chilled champagne glasses.

Yield: 7 servings

CALORIES: 87

At Tony's on Market Street in St. Louis, guests indulge in house-made pastas, seafood, veal, and prime sirloin steak. The restaurant has won the Mobil Five Star Award for the past eighteen years, and the AAA Five Diamond Award for the past five. The cuisine may be only surpassed by the pampering each guest receives from the owner, Vincent J. Bommarito.

The Ritz-Carlton
Fantino Frappé

2 canned peach halves, drained
2 canned pear halves, drained
¼ teaspoon orgeat (sweet, almond-flavored nonalcoholic syrup)
¼ ounce Coco López cream of coconut
1 splash pineapple juice
1 diamond-shaped pineapple wedge

1. Place all ingredients except pineapple piece in a blender.
2. Blend for approximately 2 minutes.
3. Fill a frappé glass with ice.
4. Pour mixture into glass.
5. Garnish with pineapple diamond.

CALORIES: 195

Manhattan's Jockey Club goes Italian. The Ritz-Carlton keeps a piece of the old Jockey Club in its new restaurant, Fantino, which is the Italian word for jockey. The Club has been completely redesigned with peach and mauve tones and French and Italian paintings. In the bar, also redecorated, bartender Norman Bukofzer continues to reign, concocting libations for Steven Bochco, cartoonist Jim Davis, and U2.

Top of the Needle Lounge
Peachsicle

2 ounces orange juice
2 ounces peach daiquiri mix
½ ounce orgeat syrup
Ice to fill tall glass
Whipped cream
1 orange slice
1 cherry

1. Place juice, mix, syrup, and ice in a blender.
2. Blend until thick.
3. Pour into a tall glass.
4. Top with whipped cream.
5. Garnish with skewered orange slice and cherry.

CALORIES: 189

70

Sightseeing can be tiresome at times—all that walking, driving, and putting up with the wily natives. For the non-squeamish there's a solution in Seattle. Only a 42-second elevator ride to the top of the Space Needle places you in the revolving Space Needle Restaurant. Partake of Pacific Northwest cuisine and nonalcoholic drinks, as Mount Rainier, the Olympic and Cascade mountain ranges, Puget Sound, Lake Union, and downtown Seattle spin by. Eighteen feet above the restaurant is the observation deck, gift shops (one-stop souvenir shopping), Space Needle construction exhibits, and the Top of the Needle Lounge.

House of Blues
Pineapple Chiffon

1½ ounces piña colada mix
½ ounce grapefruit juice
1 fresh strawberry
1 scoop ice
1 orange wheel
1 cherry

1. Place first four ingredients in blender and blend until thick.
2. Pour into a 14-ounce glass.
3. Garnish with an orange wheel and cherry.

CALORIES: 114

Opened in Cambridge, Massachusetts, in 1992 by a group of investors that includes Dan Aykroyd, the House of Blues has since added satellites in New Orleans, Los Angeles, and New York. While showcasing contemporary blues, jazz, and zydeco acts, the House pays tribute to legendary blues men with dozens of bas relief portraits in its cathedral ceiling. The three seatings for the Gospel Brunch on Sundays are often booked weeks in advance.

Buckhorn Exchange
St. Mary's Glacier

1 cup ice cubes
3 ounces pineapple juice
3 ounces coconut milk
1 orange slice
1 cherry

1. Blend first three ingredients in blender.
2. Pour into a tall highball or hurricane glass.
3. Garnish with an orange/cherry flag.

CALORIES: 273

Culinary trends come and go, but Denver's Buckhorn Exchange continues to stun patrons just as it did a century ago, with generous servings of buffalo, elk, and dry-aged beef. Opened by Henry Zietz, a scout for Buffalo Bill Cody, the restaurant maintains the Wild West flavor in the decor: more than 500 animal trophies are mounted on the walls, and a collection of 150 firearms is on display.

Club Med Sandpiper
Sandpiper Smile

4 ounces pineapple juice
1 ounce cream of coconut
1 whole medium banana
3 to 4 ounces ice
1 orange slice
1 cherry

1. Place first three ingredients and ice in blender.
2. Puree.
3. Pour drink into tall glass.
4. Garnish with umbrella skewer of orange slice and cherry.

CALORIES: 247

Notorious in the seventies and eighties for its nude beaches and wild singles nightlife, Club Med has moved into the nineties with daycare service and special activities for parents and children. With more than fifteen villages around the world, Club Med offers upscale vacations as the "antidote for civilization." Located in St. Lucie, Florida, north of Palm Beach, Club Med Sandpiper's village encompasses 500 acres with five pools, restaurants, a cocktail lounge, theater, and a disco, and activities such as golf, tennis, scuba diving, sailing, and circus workshops.

Jockey Club at the Grand Stand
The Grand Passion

2 ounces cream of coconut
4 ounces pineapple juice
1 ounce orange juice
2 ounces Hero brand rum base
1 ounce Monin passion fruit syrup
2 cups ice
1 pineapple chunk as garnish

1. Place all ingredients except the ice and pineapple garnish in a blender.
2. Now add the ice.
3. Blend well.
4. Pour mixture into a hurricane glass.
5. Garnish with pineapple chunk.

CALORIES: 227

The Grand Hotel, with 319 rooms, sits atop Mackinac Island, just north of Michigan's lower peninsula. The three-mile-long island, featured in the movie *Somewhere in Time*, is bereft of automobiles—the only way around is on horses and bicycles. When the Grand Hotel was built in 1887, it became the largest summer hotel, the world's largest pine building, and featured the world's longest porch—660 feet. The Jockey Club at the Grand Stand is located on the hotel grounds at The Jewel, the hotel's golf course.

The Greenbrier Old White Club
Punchless Piña Colada

1 ounce pineapple juice
1 ounce cream of coconut
1 teaspoon lime juice
1 cup crushed ice
1 pineapple slice
1 cherry

1. Place all ingredients except fruit in a blender and blend until smooth and creamy.
2. Pour into a Collins glass.
3. Garnish with slice of pineapple and cherry.

CALORIES: 136

Historic doesn't begin to describe The Greenbrier, located in Sulphur Springs, West Virginia. People visited in the 1700s to "take the waters," to cure any and all ailments. After the Civil War, Old White, as the resort was called, became the summer home of General Robert E. Lee. In the winter of 1941–1942, the "guests" of The Greenbrier were German and Japanese diplomats that the United States government wasn't quite sure what to do with. Later during the Second World War it became an army hospital. After the war the hotel was completely redecorated. Twenty-two United States presidents have visited the resort. And duffers such as Arnold Palmer, Bob Hope, and Bing Crosby have putted on the resort's three golf courses. Swimming, great dining, horseback riding, trout fishing, and tennis are available, as well as a return to the resort's beginnings—mineral baths at the spa and salon.

The Watergate

Cherry Blossom

2 ounces pineapple juice
2 ounces cream of
coconut
Grenadine as needed
Mint sprig

1. Chill champagne dish.
2. Fill dish with crushed ice.
3. Add pineapple juice and coconut cream.
4. Lace drink with grenadine to give appearance of streaks through the drink.
5. Garnish with mint sprig (adding the green of the tree to accent the "cherry blossoms").

CALORIES: 290

Before 1972 the Watergate Complex was famous for its world-class restaurant, bars, apartments, stores, and offices. But in 1972 the Watergate became infamous for the part it played in the downfall of a United States president. It began when the office of the Democratic National Committee in the complex was broken into and bugged. When the burglars were apprehended, they possessed a telephone number that, when dialed, rang a telephone in the White House. That direct telephone line led indirectly to the resignation of Richard Milhous Nixon.

In culinary circles, the Watergate is famous for the work of its chef, Jean-Louis Palladin, and his delectable nouvelle cuisine. The only two-star Michelin chef in the United States, he rules at the restaurant that serves international power brokers who dine overlooking the Potomac River.

Hotel Inter-Continental
Ocean Side Pool Bar & Grill
Fruit Smoothie

1 banana
½ cup pineapple
½ cup honeydew melon
½ cup cantaloupe
½ cup strawberries
¾ cup raspberries
¾ cup fresh-squeezed
  orange juice
1 scoop ice
1 strawberry

1. Place first eight ingredients in
   blender.
2. Blend until frozen.
3. Serve in a tall glass such as a Collins
   or highball glass.
4. Garnish with strawberry.

CALORIES: 204

The Ocean Side Pool Bar & Grill is situated on the fifth floor of Miami's
Inter-Continental Hotel, which overlooks Biscayne Bay and Miami Beach.
Patrons dine on fresh salads, homemade pizzas, and skewers of grilled
meats and vegetables. The bar offers a vast selection of frozen, low-
calorie tropical cocktails. The hotel's Pavillon Grill provides more formal
surroundings and an acclaimed menu of such dishes as cherry-smoked
lamb chops.

The Breakers
The Last Resort

Ice to fill ⅓ blender
¼ cantaloupe
4 ounces piña colada mix
1 fruit skewer: orange,
  cherry, pineapple, and
  strawberry

1. Fill blender ⅓ full of ice.
2. Place first two ingredients in the
   blender.
3. Blend until frozen.
4. Pour frozen mixture into a
   hurricane glass.
5. Garnish with fruit skewer.

CALORIES: 354

The Last Resort is the perfect drink to accompany the view of the Atlantic Ocean outside of the window of the Alcazar Lounge in The Breakers hotel. The seven-story Breakers, established in 1926 and listed on the National Register of Historic Places, offers a blend of old-world charm and modern convenience in Palm Beach, Florida. The hotel, with its hundred and forty acres of oceanfront grounds, features Italian Renaissance architecture with authentic fresco ceilings, and bronze and crystal Venetian chandeliers.

Kaspar's
Cinnamon Twist

4 ounces apple juice
3½ ounces apple sauce
½ cup ice
Raw sugar
Ground cinnamon

1. Place first three ingredients in blender and blend well.
2. Coat the rim of a stem glass with raw sugar.
3. Pour mixture in glass.
4. Top with a swirl of ground cinnamon.

CALORIES: 188

Gourmet magazine has lauded the creations of Seattle restaurant owner/chef's Kaspar Donier as "the best food in the city." Donier offers a creative approach to contemporary cuisine, including such signature specialties as Dungeness crab and chopped vegetable salad in sushi rolls. Another attraction: Kaspar's restaurant provides spectacular views of the Olympic Mountains, Elliott Bay, and the city's skyline.

Lee's Unleaded Blues
Easy Living

2 ounces orange juice
2 ounces grapefruit juice
2 ounces lime juice
2 ounces club soda
1 teaspoon bar sugar
2 ounces grenadine
5 to 6 ice cubes
2 cherries
2 lemon slices
2 lime slices
2 olives

1. Pour first seven ingredients into blender.
2. Blend well.
3. Pour into tall fancy glass.
4. Garnish with cherries, 1 lemon and 1 lime slice, in the glass. Garnish rim with olives, 1 lemon and 1 lime slice.

CALORIES: 265

Considered by some the best South Side blues bar in Chicago, Lee's Unleaded Blues is located in a somewhat dicey neighborhood. But inside, the atmosphere is friendly and inviting, a feeling helped immeasurably by proprietor Lee's concoctions, which are usually measured only in increments she describes as "a little bit of each."

78

Restaurant Daniel
The Fruits of Daniel

3 ounces fresh-squeezed
    orange juice
2 ounces grapefruit juice
1 ounce pineapple juice
1 tablespoon grenadine
3 mint leaves
3 strawberries
½ banana
½ tablespoon sugar
3 ice cubes
1 banana slice
1 orange slice
1 strawberry slice
1 mint sprig

1. Place first nine ingredients in a blender.
2. Blend until smooth.
3. Pour in a highball or large wine glass.
4. Garnish with a skewer of sliced banana, orange, strawberry, and mint sprig.

CALORIES: 224

Chef Daniel Boulud dazzled those who frequented Le Cirque, so when he opened his own New York restaurant, named Daniel, the chic supper crowd followed. Boulud presents seasonal French cuisine in a casual yet elegant room that evokes a French country home. Pastry chef François Payard's celebrated desserts take full advantage of fruits in season.

The Bay
Tropical Slush

3 cups water
2 cups sugar
Juice of 3 oranges
Juice of 1 lemon
3 bananas, mashed
24 ounces canned
  pineapple juice
7-Up or Sprite
Cherries, mint leaves, or
  orange wedges

1. In a 2-quart pot, boil water and sugar together until sugar is dissolved. Remove pot from heat and let cool.
2. When sugar water is cool, add juice from oranges and lemon, mashed bananas, and pineapple juice.
3. Freeze until solid.
4. Shave or chip off into tall, slender glasses.
5. Add 7-Up or Sprite to fill.
6. Serve with long spoon and thick straw.
7. Garnish with cherry, mint, or orange wedge.

Yield: about 10 servings

CALORIES: 229

In Salt Lake City, the teetotaling tradition goes back to the burg's Mormon founders. The Bay provides a lively outlet for people who wish to avoid alcohol, socialize in a nightclub for grown-ups, and perhaps do the watusi. Patrons flock to beach parties, country-music nights, and other special events on the club's three levels: a second-story dance floor, a middle-level lounge and video room, and a basement dance floor, from which it's just a few steps to a patio with a swimming pool.

Red Hot and Sassy

Virgin Marys with Plenty of Spice

The '21' Club
Virgin Mary

5 ounces Sacramento
   tomato juice
2 dashes Worcestershire
   sauce
2 dashes celery salt
Fresh pepper
Fresh lime wedge

1. Mix first two ingredients.
2. Shake well.
3. Fill whiskey sour glass with ice.
4. Pour drink over ice into the
   stemmed glass.
5. Garnish with celery salt, pepper, and
   lime wedge.

CALORIES: 36

The '21' Club, a longtime magnet for Manhattan's publishing, entertaining, and business leaders, is noted for such menu items as Chicken Hash and the '21' Hamburger. The wood-paneled clubby barroom is adorned with such memorabilia as model-size company trucks, to commemorate the executives who have bent an elbow in the bar during its six decades. Formal dining rooms are up the stairs.

The Watergate

Virgin Mary

5 ounces tomato juice
½ teaspoon horseradish
(The Watergate makes
its own horseradish
every day.)
1 drop Tabasco sauce
2 shakes Worcestershire
sauce
Powdering of cracked
rock salt and freshly
ground pepper
Pinch of celery seed
¼ teaspoon lemon juice
Lemon wedge and/or
celery stalk as garnish

1. Fill Collins glass with ice.
2. Mix all ingredients except garnishes
in the Collins glass.
3. Garnish with lemon wedge and/or
celery stalk.

CALORIES: 42

Before 1972 the Watergate Complex was famous for its world-class
restaurant, bars, apartments, stores, and offices. But in 1972 the
Watergate became infamous for the part it played in the downfall of a
United States president. It began when the office of the Democratic
National Committee in the Watergate was broken into and bugged.
When the burglars were apprehended, they possessed a telephone
number that rang a telephone in the White House. That direct
telephone line led indirectly to the resignation of Richard Milhous Nixon.

In culinary circles, the Watergate is famous for the work of its chef,
Jean-Louis Palladin, and his delectable nouvelle cuisine. The only two-star
Michelin chef in the United States, he rules at the restaurant that serves
international power brokers who dine overlooking the Potomac River.

Club Med Sandpiper

Ragin' Cajun Virgin Mary

7 ounces tomato juice
3 shakes celery salt
1 dash of A-1
1 shake Tabasco sauce
1 splash Worcestershire
  sauce
1 sprinkle freshly ground
  pepper
1 sprinkle cayenne
  pepper
1 dash horseradish
1 sprinkle dill seed
1 stalk celery

1. Fill tall glass with ice.
2. Mix all the above ingredients
   (except the celery) in the glass.
3. Garnish with a stalk of celery.

CALORIES: 71

Notorious in the seventies and eighties for its nude beaches and wild singles nightlife, Club Med has moved into the nineties with daycare service and special activities for parents and children. With more than fifteen villages around the world, Club Med offers upscale vacations as the "antidote for civilization." Located in St. Lucie, Florida, north of Palm Beach, Club Med's Sandpiper village encompasses five hundred acres with five pools, restaurants, a cocktail lounge, theater, and a disco, and activities such as golf, tennis, scuba diving, sailing, and circus workshops.

52 Stafford Street

Virgin Mary

5 ounces clamato juice
5 ounces V-8 juice
1 ounce Worcestershire sauce
8 dashes Durkee's red-hot sauce
2 ounces pickle juice (preferably dill)
1 dash lemon pepper
1 dash celery salt
1 pickle spear
2 olives
1 lemon twist
1 lime wedge

1. Place first five ingredients in shaker glass.
2. Shake well.
3. Pour into Irish-pub pint glass filled with ice.
4. Top with lemon pepper and celery salt.
5. Garnish with skewered pickle spear and 2 olives, and float a lemon twist and lime wedge in the glass.

CALORIES: 166

A beautifully restored Irish guest house in Plymouth, Wisconsin, 52 Stafford Street offers Irish music on weekend nights in autumn and winter, as well as dinner each night in its restaurant. Specialties inspired by the Old Sod include Guinness brisket, a chicken dish nicely accented with Irish Mist liqueur, and steamed mussels. The pub features a gorgeous burnished wood bar with plush seats and a friendly bartender.

Top of the Mark
The Bloody Shame

8 ounces tomato juice
1 splash Tabasco sauce
1 splash Worcestershire
  sauce
1 dash salt
1 dash pepper
1 slice lime
1 stalk celery as garnish

1. Fill a tall glass with ice.
2. Add a splash of Tabasco and Worcestershire sauce.
3. Add a dash of salt and pepper.
4. Fill the glass with tomato juice.
5. Finish the drink with a squeeze of lime.
6. Add lime piece to drink.
7. Garnish with stalk of celery.

CALORIES: 49

With an address like One Nob Hill, the Mark Hopkins Inter•Continental is the place to be in San Francisco. The hotel's nineteenth-floor penthouse, opened in 1939 as the glass-walled Top of the Mark lounge, provides a 360-degree view of the San Francisco Bay Area. The Top of the Mark gained a worldwide reputation during World War Two when hundreds of thousands of Allied servicemen shipped through San Francisco, and many used it as the real port of embarkation. Today, bartender Bert Rees uses the view for inspiration ... for great new drink ideas.

Fog City Diner
Virgin Mary

Juice of whole lemon
5 ounces tomato juice
3 ice cubes
4 dashes Worcestershire
  sauce
½ teaspoon pepper
¼ teaspoon salt
1 lemon wedge

1. Squeeze juice from lemon into shaker cup.
2. Add all remaining ingredients except the last.
3. Shake well.
4. Strain liquid into Irish coffee glass.
5. Garnish with lemon wedge.

CALORIES: 44

Although it specializes in classic diner fare, San Francisco's Fog City Diner also features inventive California cuisine. This means that a person who hankers for a chili dog and onion rings can share a table with someone who's addicted to Fog City's fabulous lobster chowder or the distinctive quesadilla with roasted hazelnuts. The exterior is aluminum paneling; inside, the booths are arranged in a long row to capture the ambiance of a railroad dining car.

Antone's
Virgin Mary

1 dash salt
1 dash pepper
1 dash Tabasco sauce
2 dashes Worcestershire sauce
¼ tablespoon horseradish
1 lime wedge
8 ounces tomato juice

1. Fill a tall glass with ice.
2. Add salt, pepper, Tabasco, Worcestershire, horseradish, and a squeeze of lime.
3. Fill the glass with tomato juice.
4. Stir well.

CALORIES: 48

John Mintz, who keeps the blues and drinks flowing, says this is his favorite recipe for a Bloody Mary. Antone's, in Austin, Texas, is nationally known as a premier rhythm and blues club. Big blues names such as Muddy Waters and B. B. King have frequented the club. And the music is king at this no-frills bar. It may look like your feet will stick to the floor, but they won't be stuck long. The music will get your feet tapping until, finally, you won't be able to fight it any longer, and you'll find yourself on the dance floor.

Douglas Dunes Sir Douglas Cafe
Bloody Mary

Celery salt
3 ounces Bloody Mary
  mix
1 dash pepper
1 dash dill sauce
2 lime slices

1. Rim a large rocks glass with celery salt.
2. Fill glass with ice.
3. Add ingredients, squeezing 1 lime slice for juice, and then add slice to drink.
4. Garnish with other lime slice.

CALORIES: 34

Located in West Michigan, the Saugatuck-Douglas area is a haven for Chicago and Detroit tourists who flock to the former artists' colony for its unique shops and beautiful, sandy Lake Michigan beaches. Douglas Dunes is a popular resort featuring rooms and cottages, an excellent restaurant, and six bars, ranging from a loud and crazy bar with dance music to the quiet poolside lounge.

The Inn at Little Washington

Virgin Mary

6 ounces Campbell's
  tomato juice
4 dashes Worcestershire
  sauce
2 dashes Tabasco sauce
¼ teaspoon celery salt
½ teaspoon fresh
  horseradish
Juice of ¼ lime
1 celery stalk

1. Put first six ingredients in a shaker
   cup.
2. Shake well.
3. Pour over ice into highball glass.
4. Garnish with celery stalk.

CALORIES: 65

Pretty soon the drowsy town of Washington, Virginia, will need to install its first stoplight to slow the traffic speeding toward The Inn at Little Washington. Only The Inn glitters with *all* of the most coveted awards: five stars from the Mobil Travel Guide, five diamonds from AAA, the DiRoNa award, Restaurant of the Year honors from the James Beard Foundation for 1993, and . . . well, you get the idea. Getting a reservation is another matter: The Inn's twelve rooms are booked a year in advance.

Just Desserts

After-Dinner Drinks Featuring
Coffee, Chocolate, Ice Cream,
and Oreo Cookies

Restaurant at The Little Nell
Hot Minted Cocoa

4 tablespoons cocoa
  powder
1 cup brewed coffee
1 quart milk
½ cup sugar
2 tablespoons chopped
  fresh mint leaves
¾ cup whipping cream

1. Liquify cocoa powder in a 2-quart mixing bowl with about ¼ cup of the coffee until it forms a smooth paste.
2. Heat milk, sugar, mint leaves, and remaining coffee together until mixture comes to a boil.
3. Remove immediately and slowly add to the cocoa paste, stirring constantly.
4. Allow mixture to set for 2 minutes. Meanwhile, whip the cream until thick.
5. Strain the hot cocoa through a fine strainer to remove the mint.
6. Gently fold the whipped cream into the strained liquid and serve immediately in warmed mugs.
7. Garnish, if desired, with fresh mint sprigs.

Yield: 4 servings

CALORIES: 161

Since its opening in 1989, the Restaurant at The Little Nell Hotel in Aspen, Colorado, has seen honors pile up like a Rocky Mountain snowfall. Executive chef George Mahaffey's American alpine innovations have been recognized with a DiRoNa award, and the luxurious restaurant was ranked among the top ten by *Restaurants & Institutions* magazine.

Key Largo
Monastery Coffee

1 teaspoon hazelnut
Italian syrup
1 teaspoon Irish cream
Italian syrup
6 ounces brewed coffee
4 tablespoons whipped
cream
1 dash nutmeg

1. Pour both syrups into coffee mug.
2. Add coffee to fill.
3. Top with whipped cream.
4. Dust with nutmeg.

CALORIES: 67

Iced Coffee Nudge

4 to 5 ice cubes
1 teaspoon Amaretto
Italian syrup
1 teaspoon Irish cream
Italian syrup
6 ounces brewed coffee
4 tablespoons whipped
cream
Dash cinnamon

1. Fill a coffee mug with ice cubes.
2. Pour both syrups into mug.
3. Add coffee to fill.
4. Top with whipped cream and a
dusting of cinnamon.

CALORIES: 62

Coffee Mocha

1 teaspoon crème de
cocoa Italian syrup
6 ounces brewed coffee
(hot or cold, your
preference)
4 tablespoons whipped
cream
1 dash chocolate powder

1. Pour syrup into coffee mug.
2. Add coffee to fill. (Fill mug or glass
with ice first, if you are making this
as an iced drink.)
3. Top with whipped cream.
4. Dust with chocolate.

CALORIES: 47

Variation: 1 teaspoon Chocolate Mint Italian syrup for Key Largo Coffee Minty Mocha Coffee. Calories: 59

Key Largo restaurant and nightclub is known for nightly performances by some of Portland's best R & B, blues, and rock and roll bands, as well as occasional bookings of nationally known jazz acts. Caribbean decor updates Key Largo's setting in a landmark brick building in the city's Historic Old Town neighborhood.

Jake's Famous Crawfish Restaurant
Iced Mocha Coffee

1 ounce Hershey's
  Chocolate Syrup
10 ounces double-
  strength coffee
1 splash half and half
5 to 6 ice cubes

1. Pour the first three ingredients into a pint glass.
2. Place stainless-steel shaker over pint glass and secure a tight seal. (A shaker cup can be used for steps 2 and 3.)
3. Shake vigorously at least 8 times (a back-and-forth piston motion performed over one's shoulder).
4. Pour from shaker into pint glass over ice.

CALORIES: 86

In Portland, Oregon, Jake's Famous Crawfish has been serving fish-house specials with a flair since 1892. Diners can choose from more than thirty seafood entrées, and can order one of several types of oysters by specifying the Pacific Northwest bay where they are harvested. While the fish is fresh, the setting is a throwback: Waiters are garbed in white service coats, and the dining rooms are done in brass, wood, and stained glass. Jake's popular drinks are made without shortcuts or blenders. Bowls of fruit adorn the bar, and the staff cuts and squeezes fresh lemons, limes, or oranges for every citrus drink.

The Maisonette
Café Au Chocolate

6 ounces of hot, strong, brewed coffee

1 ounce half and half

1 teaspoon unsweetened cocoa powder

¾ ounce simple syrup, or to taste

⅛ teaspoon cinnamon

1 ounce whipped heavy cream

1 tablespoon chocolate shavings

1 cinnamon stick

1. Combine first 5 ingredients in stemmed glass or mug.
2. Mix well.
3. Garnish with whipped heavy cream, chocolate shavings, and cinnamon stick.

CALORIES: 305

After The Maisonette received its twenty-eighth consecutive Five Star Award recently—a streak that no other American restaurant can match—one would be tempted to think the management had little left to prove. But chef Georges Haidon's French and northern Italian cuisine, an extensive and thoughtful wine list, and a sophisticated ambience all combine to suggest that this Cincinnati treasure will be honored for years to come.

The American Club
Cafe American Club

1 ounce nonalcoholic
  peppermint schnapps
1 scoop vanilla ice cream
6 ounces iced cappuccino
Whipped cream
Chocolate shavings
1 peppermint stick

1. Place first three ingredients in a blender.
2. Blend until smooth.
3. Pour into a stemmed glass.
4. Garnish with whipped cream, chocolate shavings, and peppermint stick.

CALORIES: 175

With all that corn and wheat in the Midwest, there's room for only one AAA Five Diamond resort hotel. It's the American Club, in Kohler, Wisconsin. Located within the resort, The Horse and Plow offers soup, salad, sandwiches, and heartier fare for both dinner and lunch. Food or drinks are served in a tavern-style restaurant, decorated in dark-colored woods, glittering brass, sparkling stained glass, and booths for both comfort and privacy.

Second City
Virgin Piña Colada

1 scoop vanilla ice cream
2 ounces cream or whole
  milk
3 ounces coconut milk
3 ounces pineapple juice
1 orange slice
1 cherry

1. Place first four ingredients in a blender.
2. Blend until a smooth consistency is achieved.
3. Pour into a bubble glass.
4. Garnish with skewered orange slice and cherry.

CALORIES: 227

Second City, with clubs in Chicago, Toronto, and Detroit, has launched the comic careers of Joan Rivers, John Candy, Dan Aykroyd, Bill Murray, Shelley Long, and many other funny people. Comedy revues consist of satirical musical numbers, quick blackouts, extended sketches, and improv sessions based on audience suggestions. A variety of drinks and snacks are available before and during the show. Among those who started their stage careers by serving cocktails at Second City are playwright David Mamet and actress Catherine O'Hara.

Blackwolf Run Clubhouse
Pineapple Float

4 ounces pineapple juice
5 large ice cubes
1 large scoop vanilla ice cream
Pieces of pineapple
Cherries

1. Place pineapple juice and ice in blender.
2. Blend well.
3. Place scoop of ice cream in a tall glass.
4. Pour blender mixture over ice cream.
5. Garnish with pineapple and cherries on a pick.

CALORIES: 144

The bar at Blackwolf Run Golf Course in Kohler, Wisconsin, overlooks the Sheboygan River. If you prefer your water in a glass instead of a hazard, the main dining room offers a panoramic view of the golf course. It also has a huge fieldstone fireplace and loft area, and for a feel of the outside indoors, there's a glass-walled dining porch. The view is of one of the two Pete Dye–designed championship eighteen-hole courses; this spectacular River course was named among the top four public courses in the nation by *Golf Digest*'s list of "America's 100 Greatest Golf Courses."

The Marc
Monkey Nuts

2 scoops vanilla ice cream
½ ounce hazelnut syrup
½ ounce Coco López cream of coconut
1 splash pineapple juice
1 dash ground nutmeg

1. Place first four ingredients in a blender.
2. Blend until creamy.
3. Serve in a poco grande glass.
4. Garnish with nutmeg

CALORIES: 371

The Marc's owner and chef, Andrew Marc Rothschild, brings classic French influences to his American cafe in Chicago, resulting in an array of meat, poultry, and seafood dishes enhanced with light sauces and infused oils. Among the winsome offerings is a napoleon of striped bass with champagne vinaigrette. The 110-seat dining room is notable for its Mission furniture, high windows swaddled in gauze, and striking floral arrangements.

Restaurant at The Little Nell
Tootsie Pop Shake

½ ripe banana
6 ounces fresh-squeezed orange juice
1 full jigger Hershey's chocolate syrup
2 full scoops vanilla ice cream
3 ice cubes

1. Place all ingredients in a blender.
2. Blend until smooth.
3. Pour into brandy snifter.

CALORIES: 554

Since its opening in 1989, the Restaurant at The Little Nell Hotel in Aspen has seen honors pile up like a Rocky Mountain snowfall. Executive chef George Mahaffey's American alpine innovations have been recognized with a DiRoNa award, and the luxurious restaurant was ranked among the top ten by *Restaurants & Institutions* magazine.

Charley's Crab GR Steamer Bar
Banana Nut Shake

3 ounces milk
2 cups vanilla ice cream
2 tablespoons pecan
   pieces
1 ripe banana
1 teaspoon vanilla extract
2 ounces milk
1 dab whipped cream
1 banana slice

1. Place all ingredients except whipped cream and banana slice in a blender in the order listed.
2. Blend well.
3. Pour into a tall pilsner glass.
4. Garnish with whipped cream and a banana slice.

CALORIES: 663

Charley's Crab, located in the heart of President Jerry Ford's hometown, is known throughout western Michigan for serving exceptionally fresh seafood. Overlooking the Grand River, in downtown Grand Rapids, Michigan, the restaurant and bar offer plenty of windows from which to watch the river meander by, and a patio for warm weather service. Within the restaurant, the GR Steamer Bar serves up lighter fare—pastas and sandwiches—and live jazz nightly.

Oliver's Review
Oreo Cookie

Ice cubes to fill a 16-
   ounce glass
6 Oreo cookies
1 scoop vanilla ice cream
1 cup milk
Whipped cream

1. Fill a 16-ounce glass with ice.
2. Place ice in a blender.
3. Add cookies, ice cream, and milk.
4. Mix to semi-creamy texture.
5. Pour into 16-ounce glass.
6. Garnish with a dab of whipped cream.

CALORIES: 443

Brown University students flock to Oliver's Review, in Providence, Rhode Island. The blaring juke box provides background music for some of the best pub food on the Eastern Seaboard. Oliver's Review has two bars, the more sedate found downstairs. The upstairs bar serves patrons while they shoot pool in the game room.

Daisy Buchanan's
Frozen Oreo Cookie

2 scoops very soft vanilla
   ice cream
1 scoop ice
2 Oreo cookies
1 tablespoon Hershey
   syrup

1. Fill blender ⅓ full with ice.
2. Place ice cream and Oreo cookies
   in the blender.
3. Blend for several seconds only.
4. Pour syrup into a 12-ounce glass so
   that it coats the sides.
5. Pour blender mixture into glass.
6. If preferred, garnish with more
   Oreo cookies.

CALORIES: 294

Once part of Boston's Charles River tidal flat, the area known as Back Bay was filled with dirt in the 1800s, and soon was filled with houses of Boston's elite. Such is the locale of Daisy Buchanan's bar, named for a character in F. Scott Fitzgerald's book *The Great Gatsby*. At the bar, players from the Boston Celtics, Bruins, or Red Sox may be found, along with a smattering of movie and music personalities. Larry Bird, Jim Rice, Scott Cooper, and Lenny Kravitz have passed through the bar's door, which was taken from the old city hall.

The Cactus Rose at Rancho Encantado
Orange Sunset

1¾ ounces nonalcoholic
   peach schnapps or
   flavoring
2 ounces fresh-squeezed
   orange juice
1 ounce cranberry juice
1 splash club soda
1 cherry
1 slice fresh peach

1. Fill tall frosted glass with ice.
2. Add the next three ingredients.
3. Stir gently.
4. Add splash of club soda.
5. Garnish with a skewered cherry and
   fresh peach-slice flag.

CALORIES: 90

Unhindered views of the sunset over the Rio Grande Valley to the Jemez Mountains provide a magical dinner accompaniment at Rancho

Encantado, an intimate guest ranch in the foothills of the Sangre de Cristo Mountains, twelve miles north of Santa Fe, New Mexico. The restaurant's menu features fine cuts of beef, lamb, and pork. The bar offers several nonalcoholic drinks invented by beverage manager Mamie Gallegos, who is a teetotaler.

Four Seasons Hotel
Santa's Maui Vacation

3 ounces pineapple juice
1 ounce Coco López coconut syrup
½ ripe banana
1 splash grenadine
1 splash sweet-and-sour mix
4 ounces ice
1 chocolate chip/ macadamia nut cookie
1 chocolate-dipped "tuxedo" strawberry
1 candy cane

1. Place first 6 ingredients in a blender.
2. Blend until smooth.
3. Serve in large bubble glass.
4. Garnish with cookie, strawberry, and candy cane.

CALORIES: 306

In Houston, Texas, the Four Seasons Hotel's DeVille Restaurant gives high-end business travelers a reason to return for pleasure: chef Tony Ruppe's cooking, which includes a remarkable salmon dish cured with tequila. The four-diamond luxury hotel's Lobby Lounge welcomes fatigued travelers with comfortable chairs, a pianist, and a bar that serves the drink on this page, which won first place in AAA's Zero-Proof Mix-Off Competition. Held every holiday season, the competition challenges Houston's four-diamond restaurants to create the city's best non-alcoholic drink.

Old Havana Docks Lounge
Afternoon Delight

Ice to fill Collins glass
5 ounces peach ice
  cream
2 ounces orange juice
1 orange slice

1. Fill a Collins glass with ice and place that ice in blender.
2. Then put ice cream and orange juice in the blender.
3. Mix until well blended.
4. Pour back into the Collins glass.
5. Garnish with orange slice.

CALORIES: 156

Summer Strawberry

4 ounces strawberry
  puree
1 ounce ice cream
1 ounce orange juice
1 ounce piña colada mix
Ice to fill tall glass
1 orange slice
1 strawberry

1. Place all ingredients except the orange slice and strawberry in a blender.
2. Add enough ice to fill a tall glass, and blend until smooth.
3. Pour into a tall glass.
4. Garnish with orange slice and strawberry.

CALORIES: 201

Every sunset in Key West, Florida, is an event, where jugglers, singers, mimes, food vendors, and souvenir hawkers gather at Mallory Square. All applaud when the last of the sun's rays fall beyond the horizon. A perfect place to avoid the mob but still enjoy the event is at the Havana Docks Lounge, at the Pier House. The lounge, an old William R. Porter docks shipping office, comes to life with music and dancing. Another great place to enjoy the Key West life-style and weather is outdoors at the Beach Club.

Williamsburg Inn
Froth Punch

2 tablespoons Coco López cream of coconut

2 ounces orange juice

2 ounces cranberry or pineapple juice

2 ounces ginger ale

2 scoops raspberry sorbet or sherbet

2 tablespoons whipped cream

1 tablespoon shaved chocolate

1 cherry

1. Place first five ingredients in a blender.
2. Blend well.
3. Pour into hurricane glass.
4. Top with whipped cream, shaved chocolate, and cherry.

CALORIES: 374

Guests of the Williamsburg Inn, in Williamsburg, Virginia, can choose from 300 wines, several cognacs, and many nonalcoholic refreshments in the five-star hotel's lounges. Built in 1932, the inn has preserved its stately Regency decor while updating its amenities to include a health club for hotel guests, and contemporary kitchens and bathrooms in the nearby Colonial homes that are also available for rent.

Bossa Nova
Mango Mambo Freeze

8 ounces mango sorbet
½ ounce fresh lime juice
¾ ounce fresh-squeezed
orange juice
1 lime wheel

1. Place first three ingredients in a blender.
2. Blend until smooth and slightly liquefied.
3. Pour into an oversize (10-ounce) martini glass.
4. Garnish with fresh lime wheel.

CALORIES: 230

Bossa Nova seduces the hip Chicago crowd with its diverse selection of international *tapas*, small portions of exemplary edibles with influences that range from the American Midwest to the East Orient. Live music—Latin, jazz, and reggae—provides the perfect background beat for marathon dining as well as kinetic dancing.

The Old House Restaurant
Tiger's Tail

4 ounces plain yogurt
4 ounces mango juice
1 ounce cranberry juice
1 ounce lemonade
½ cup crushed ice
1 orange slice
1 cherry

1. Pour the first five ingredients into a blender.
2. Blend until smooth.
3. Pour into a hurricane glass.
4. Garnish with skewered orange slice and cherry.

CALORIES: 179

The fine dining at Santa Fe's posh Eldorado Hotel's The Old House features extraordinary seafood specials, including an award-winning swordfish recipe, rack of lamb, grilled veal, and free-range chicken prepared by chefs trained at the world's best culinary institutes.

Hotel Bel-Air
Smoothie

5 fresh strawberries
4 ounces fresh-squeezed orange juice
4 ounces pineapple juice
4 ounces half and half
2 tablespoons plain yogurt
2 ounces honey
2 ounces Trader Vic's Koko Kreme Syrup (coconut flavor)
1 ounce grenadine
1 whole banana
Skewered fruit pieces

1. Place all ingredients in a blender filled ⅓ full of crushed ice.
2. Blend ingredients.
3. Pour into a 14-ounce hurricane glass.
4. Garnish with skewered fruit pieces.
5. Serve with a long straw.

CALORIES: 856

Gary Cooper, Greta Garbo, Grace Kelly, Gregory Peck, Marilyn Monroe, and the Kennedy and Rockefeller families have all made The Hotel Bel-Air their home away from home. On Los Angeles's west side, the fashionable Bel Air district had its beginnings on the hotel grounds, where real estate developer Alfonzo E. Bell built his sales offices in the 1920s. Bell subdivided the foothills north of Sunset Boulevard and laid out roads to develop the neighborhood. In the early forties, Bell's offices and stables were bought and converted to hotel accommodations. The Bar, where Howard Hughes once procured multimillion-dollar business deals, features wood paneling, a fireplace, a baby grand piano, and nightly entertainment.

The Boulders Resort
Smooth Desert Dream

3 ounces strawberry
daiquiri mix

3 ounces banana daiquiri
mix

1½ ounces whole, 2
percent, or skim milk

1½ ounces nonfat yogurt

1 ounce Sprite or 7-Up

1 strawberry

1. Place all ingredients except
   strawberry in a blender.
2. Blend until smooth.
3. Pour over ice into a 16-ounce
   plastic glass (if you're drinking
   poolside).
4. Garnish with a strawberry.

CALORIES: 416

The Boulders can refer to rocks or a resort. Found in Carefree, Arizona, both are unique in their own way. In the Sonoran Desert north of Phoenix, the rocks are a strange and special outcropping of granite boulders that are 12 million years old. The Boulders has been named one of the top twenty resorts on the mainland by *Condé Nast Traveler* and Andrew Harper's *Hideaway Report*. Built to reflect the sand and rocks of the desert, The Boulders features guest casitas, restaurants, and a main lodge—decorated with the colors and materials of the desert—as well as award-winning golf courses, pools, and tennis courts.

Doug's Body Shop
Banana Milkshake

1 medium banana	1. Place all ingredients in a blender.
½ pint milk	2. Add 1 cup ice.
1 tablespoon honey	3. Blend well.
1 cup ice	4. Serve in a Collins or tall glass.

CALORIES: 217

Auto aficionados will feel they have died and gone to car heaven. People who just enjoy eating good food in a joint with a fun atmosphere won't feel too bad either. At Doug's Body Shop, in Ferndale in the Detroit area, you may dine in a '52 Edsel, '58 Packard, '60 Chrysler, '64 T Bird, or a '65 Mercedes. Cars line the walls like booths, with tables inside the cars. Walls are filled with hub caps, road signs, and other auto memorabilia. Lunch in a T Bird, or have dinner in an Edsel. Shift into overdrive to dance to the driving beat of Top 40, jazz, rock, or R & B.

Top of the Needle Lounge
Mt. Rainier

Ice to fill tall glass	1. Fill tall glass with ice, and place that ice in blender.
3 ounces half and half	
2 ounces crème de cacao syrup	2. Then place first four ingredients in the blender.
½ ounce hazelnut syrup	3. Blend until thick.
½ ounce Irish cream syrup	4. Pour into a tall or squall glass.
Whipped cream	5. Top with whipped cream and shaved chocolate.
Shaved chocolate	

CALORIES: 418

Sightseeing can be tiresome at times—all that walking, driving, and putting up with the wily natives. For the non-squeamish there's a solution in Seattle. Only a 42-second elevator ride to the top of the Space Needle places you in the revolving Space Needle Restaurant.

Partake of Pacific Northwest cuisine and nonalcoholic drinks, as Mount Rainier, the Olympic and Cascade mountain ranges, Puget Sound, Lake Union, and downtown Seattle spin by. Eighteen feet above the restaurant is the observation deck, gift shops (one-stop souvenir shopping), Space Needle construction exhibits, and drinks at the Top of the Needle Lounge.

Pinehurst Resort
Colorado Bulldog (No Teeth)

¾ ounce nonalcoholic crème de cacao
2 ounces half and half
3 ounces cola
1 ounce club soda
1 dab whipped cream
Chocolate shavings

1. Fill a shaker cup with ice.
2. Pour in crème de cacao and half and half.
3. Add cola to shaker cup.
4. Top with club soda.
5. Shake.
6. Pour liquid in a 10-ounce Collins glass filled with ice.
7. Garnish with whipped cream and chocolate shavings.

CALORIES: 169

With its seven championship golf courses, Pinehurst Resort and Country Club is one of America's most famous golf havens. Nicknamed "The Queen of the South," the resort boasts 510 deluxe accommodations, more than 20 tennis courts, carriage rides, and a full marina. *Bon Appétit* considers it one of the top resorts in the United States. Golfers and nongolfers alike relax in the Ryder Cup Lounge.

Hotel Del Coronado
Orange Avenue Fizz

4 ounces orange juice
2 ounces half and half
1 egg white
¼ cup crushed ice
1 ounce club soda
1 orange slice

1. Pour all ingredients except club soda into a blender.
2. Blend on high speed for 10 seconds.
3. Pour mixture into a poco grande glass.
4. Add soda to the top of the drink.
5. Do not stir.
6. Garnish with an orange slice on the rim of the glass.

CALORIES: 142

Those in the know say the Prince of Wales met Coronado housewife Wallis Simpson for the first time in the Hotel Del Coronado's Ballroom. The Prince, who became King Edward VIII, later abdicated his throne for Simpson. The Hotel Del Coronado has accommodated fourteen U.S. presidents at some point in their careers, from Benjamin Harrison to Bill Clinton. "The Del," resting on the Coronado peninsula, across the bay from San Diego, is one of the world's most grand and elegant wooden Victorian hotels. The original five-story structure opened in 1888; it has since served as a location for such movies as *Some Like It Hot*, with Jack Lemmon, Tony Curtis, and Marilyn Monroe, and *The Stunt Man*, with Peter O'Toole. Nonalcoholic drinks, as well as the atmosphere, may be soaked up at the Palm Court Lounge.

The Crown Room
Crown Calypso

Ice to fill ⅓ blender
½ small banana
1½ ounces cream
1 ounce orange juice
½ ounce simple syrup
1 banana chunk
1 mint sprig

1. Fill blender ⅓ full of ice.
2. Place banana, cream, orange juice, and syrup in blender.
3. Blend well.
4. Pour mixture in a tall glass.
5. Garnish with a banana chunk and sprig of mint.

CALORIES: 170

Built in 1907, San Francisco's historic Fairmont Hotel, and its Crown Room, has served ten United States presidents, world leaders, and countless royalty. The Garden Room of the Fairmont hosted dignitaries as they drafted the charter for the United Nations. The Fairmont also provided the setting for the television series "Hotel."

The Ivy Grill
Strawberry Shortcake

1½ cups ice
¾ cup strawberries
¼ cup cream
2 tablespoons almond syrup
2 tablespoons whipped cream
1 dash nutmeg

1. Place first four ingredients in a blender.
2. Blend until smooth.
3. Pour into a poco grande glass.
4. Top with whipped cream and a dusting of nutmeg.

CALORIES: 423

Owned by Dartmouth College, The Hanover Inn is New Hampshire's oldest hotel. Students, faculty, alumni, and locals frequent its Ivy Grill for contemporary American cuisine in an Art Deco setting, or, in warm weather, on the terrace. For more elaborate fare in a formal atmosphere, they dine at the inn's Daniel Webster Room.

The Regent

Coconut Lips

2 ounces cranberry juice
2 ounces pineapple juice
1 ounce heavy cream
½ ounce cream of
coconut
1 sprinkle grenadine

1. Fill a shaker with ice.
2. Pour all ingredients except the grenadine into shaker.
3. Shake well.
4. Strain into a tall glass.
5. Sprinkle with grenadine.

CALORIES: 202

Among those who have enjoyed being pampered at The Regent Beverly Wilshire in Beverly Hills, California, are Warren Beatty, Michael Eisner, the Prince of Wales, Princess Anne, Prince Andrew, Princess Margaret, King Hussein of Jordan, presidents Carter, Ford, and Reagan, King Olav of Norway, and the Dalai Lama. One of the most popular "rooms" at the luxury hotel, located on Wilshire and Rodeo, is the Presidential Suite. The six-room suite has been the palace-away-from-palace for Woolworth heiress Barbara Hutton, Elvis Presley, Ringo Starr, and singer Elton John, and has provided the set for Richard Gere and Julia Roberts in the film *Pretty Woman*. The price . . . $4,000 per night.

S.O.B.'s
Banana Lemonade

6 ice cubes
4 teaspoons honey
2 tablespoons water
2 small fresh mint leaves
1 large banana
¼ cup fresh lemon juice
Lemon slices
Extra mint leaf

1. Place first six ingredients in a blender.
2. Blend until smooth.
3. Fill a 12-ounce glass with ice.
4. Pour mixture into glass.
5. Garnish with lemon and mint.

CALORIES: 169

By the border of the West Village and Soho in New York City floats the tropical island known as S.O.B.'s. With the hottest reggae, Latin, Caribbean, Calypso, Cajun, and Brazilian samba music, S.O.B.'s, or Sounds of Brazil, features dancing, exotic tropical drinks, thatched bars, painted vines creeping down columns, and huge parrots swinging from perches overhead.

Waterway Cafe
Hawaiian Banana Swirl

3 ounces banana daiquiri
  mix
1 ounce pineapple juice
1 ounce papaya juice
Whipped cream
Chocolate sauce
1 banana slice

1. Fill a blender ⅓ full of ice.
2. Add daiquiri mix and juices.
3. Blend until smooth and pour into a
   tall glass.
4. Garnish with whipped cream,
   chocolate sauce, and banana slice.
5. Chocolate sauce may also be
   swirled around the inside of the
   glass before pouring in the drink.

CALORIES: 242

Palm Beach, Florida, may be pretentious, but the Waterway Cafe in Palm Beach Gardens isn't. On the waterfront, surrounded by tropical scenery, diners delight in the fresh seafood and friendly service at the open-air restaurant. It's a favorite with locals. And on Sundays and Wednesdays the Cafe cranks up the reggae music. People dance across a bridge to a floating bar, decorated with life preservers, to order their favorite nonalcoholic drink.

Cunard QE 2
Royal Mocktail

½ small banana
2 strawberries
1 ounce cream of coconut
1½ ounces pineapple juice
½ cup ice
1 dash grenadine
1 extra strawberry
1 small Union Jack flag on cocktail stick

1. Place all ingredients except the grenadine, extra strawberry, and Union Jack flag in a blender.
2. Blend until smooth and creamy.
3. Pour into a hurricane glass.
4. Drizzle grenadine over the top of the drink.
5. Place 1 strawberry and flag on top for garnish.

CALORIES: 207

During the summer of 1993, Prince Edward visited the *Queen Elizabeth 2*. So as not to serve just any old drink, Roger Metcalf, bartender at the Queens Grill on the *QE 2*, and honorary life member of the United Kingdom Bartenders Guild, concocted a special elixir, the Royal Mocktail.

The Fiddlehead
Fiddlehead House Tea

4 ounces whole rose hips tea

3 ounces chamomile tea

1 ounce mint tea

1 sprig mint per serving

1. Mix first three ingredients in a measuring cup, then place the mixture into a coffee filter.
2. Using a pour-through coffee maker, pour boiling water over the tea grounds into a pot.
3. To double-brew, pour the liquid tea through the tea grounds over a second pot.
4. Serve in coffee mugs, with a sprig of fresh mint in each.

Yield: one pot of tea

CALORIES: 0

Named in honor of a sweet-tasting fern that sprouts in nearby forests, The Fiddlehead Restaurant and Bakery emphasizes food that is "close to the earth," accompanied by homemade bread made from organic flours. Opened in 1978, the Fiddlehead's location in Juneau, Alaska, isolates it from the suppliers that serve restaurants in the lower forty-eight. One solution: The owners lease a plot of local farmland to grow such crops as the rhubarb used in its celebrated pies. Less easy to find locally are the three herbal teas used in the very popular, caffeine-free Fiddlehead House Tea; they arrive via barge from Seattle.

Grapes
Without Wrath

A Guide to Dealcoholized Wines

The Taste of Yesterday

"It's just grape juice, isn't it?" was a question often heard in conversations about wine without alcohol. Until the early 1980s, it was mostly true: The nonalcoholic "wine" found on shelves was grape juice trying to look like wine with *faux* labels and bottles. This sweet juice was not without its supporters, but people who didn't read the label carefully were disappointed.

Some nonalcoholic wine was made in the early to mid-1980s, however, using a cold-stabilization process. The taste wasn't "wine-ish," but thin and watery. It even lost most of its similarities to grape juice.

Then the health-conscious in the mid-eighties demanded more. Entrepreneurs saw an opening—nonalcoholic wine with all the characteristics of real wine but without the drawbacks—i.e., the alcohol. With people drinking less alcohol for a number of reasons—pregnancy, prescription drugs, business lunches, religion, more responsible attitudes about driving, and concerns about caloric intake—a good nonalcoholized wine could ride high on the health-craze wave.

New or improved processes to remove the alcohol made a big difference in the taste. With the new processes came a new title. Wine without alcohol went from nonalcoholic to dealcoholized. Perhaps because the title had an unwanted association to juices that were labeled "nonalcoholic," it became *de rigueur* to call the new offerings dealcoholized wine.

Whereas beer without the alcohol can not be marketed as beer, wine without alcohol can still be called wine. The Federal Bureau of Alcohol, Tobacco & Firearms, which controls labeling, ruled that biteless beer (containing less than 0.5 percent alcohol) can only be called brew, or another non-beer name. The ruling did not address the labeling of dealcoholized wine, which also contains less than 0.5 percent alcohol. (This amount is no higher than the percentage of alcohol found in most freshly squeezed orange juices.) Removing the alcohol also removes approximately half the calories, which is another plus for the health-conscious.

Now one can find a wide variety of dealcoholized wines, from Chardonnay to Zinfandel, in hues ranging from the pale, strawlike yellow of a Chablis to the deep garnet red of a Cabernet Sauvignon. The options have increased dramatically.

The Taste of Today

Almost everyone—including even the producers of nonalcoholic wine—agrees that dedicated wine drinkers who are looking for the subtleness of a California Chardonnay or an Oregon Pinot Noir will not find it in the taste of dealcoholized wine.

"The very sophisticated wine drinkers don't grasp the concept," says Stanley Hock of Sutter Home Winery, which produces Sutter Home Frē, a nationally distributed dealcoholized wine. "The less frequent wine drinkers are very intrigued by it and see a place for it. The market is for the less sophisticated wine drinker."

"Sophisticated" wine drinkers have problems drinking nonalcoholic wine because, well, it doesn't have alcohol. Alcohol in wine provides some of the weight or density, which gives wine a very specific feel in the mouth. That "mouthfeel" just isn't there with dealcoholized wine. Sophisticated wine drinkers also miss what is lost in the wine's personality during and after the alcohol removal. Wine is a complex creature, a living thing. It doesn't respond well to being ripped apart.

"We call dealcoholized wine a 'wine alternative,' " says Doug Welsch, winemaker at the Fenn Valley Vineyards, in Fennville, Michigan. "It's not a replacement, but an alternative to wine."

William Leigon, vice-president of Ariél Vineyards, one of

the largest producers of dealcoholized wine, agrees. "The use of dealcoholized wine is event-oriented: a party, people out in public. We do sixty percent of our sales at the end of the year, because of the five major holidays. Not a lot of people take it home for dinner."

So who drinks dealcoholized wine? "Our drinker has a somewhat similar profile to that of a regular wine drinker," says Ariél's Leigon. "Our drinker has a higher income, higher education, and is a college graduate. The difference is they tend to be older, thirty-five and up. Wine drinkers are twenty-five and up. People in their forties and fifties are the bulk of our drinkers. They're primarily female (at least 60 to 65 percent) with the exception of Cabernet drinkers, who are 70 to 80 percent male. The one thing that links them is the belief that somehow alcohol can be detrimental to their health. It's a real large cross section."

Sutter Home's Hock agrees. "We think the audience for it varies. It's people looking for an alcohol-free alternative for a business lunch or for a dinner party, to take care of guests. But they still have a taste for wine."

A "taste" of wine perhaps isn't enough for the serious wine drinkers, whose palates are accustomed to more expensive and complicated wine. But those who drink more "economical" wine, and have more flexible palates, may find it to be an acceptable compromise. And, as an alternative to wine, some of the nonalcoholic wines are quite palatable, especially the sparkling wines. Another plus: Dealcoholized winemaking is in its infancy, and the improvements are bound to continue. In just the past decade, the progress has been amazing.

Removing the alcohol from wine has become quite a science. Two basic methods are being used: reverse osmosis or membrane filtration; and spinning cone column. Two of the largest producers of dealcoholized wine each use a different method, and both claim its process makes its wine better.

Ariél Vineyards

Ariél's claim to fame is the winning of a gold medal for its Ariél Blanc in a blind tasting at the 1986 Los Angeles County Fair. The gold medal has been a coup for marketing the wine, because the Blanc was chosen over wines *with* alcohol.

It's an event that won't likely be repeated; the red-faced judges created a new category to single out the wines with alcohol from those without.

Leigon says he knows the reason for Ariél's success—the process. "We hold two patents on the cold-filtration process. The wine is never heated. All the others heat it up."

The cold-filtration process, called reverse osmosis, begins with the wine in a tank. The wine is then pumped through cylinders with membranes that separate alcohol and water from the wine, leaving a concentrate. The water and alcohol go into a separate tank, and the wine concentrate is refiltered ten to twenty times. After the alcohol has been removed, the wine "essence" is then reconstituted with water and grape juice.

Leigon also gives credit to more than the process. "We use good grapes. We're dedicated. Making dealcoholized wine is all we do."

Beginning humbly in 1985 with the production of 1,574 cases of Blanc, Ariél grew rapidly, with sales zooming to 143,608 cases in 1992. Its wine, sold in more than twenty countries, includes Blanc, White Zinfandel, Cabernet Sauvignon, Napa Valley Cabernet Sauvignon, Rouge, oak-aged Chardonnay, Johannesburg Riesling, Napa Chardonnay, Cabernet Franc, and sparkling Brut, *méthode champenoise* Prospero Blanc de Blanc, and Celebration.

Ariél wines conform to the Heart Smart standards of the FDA, and carry the Heart Smart Seal.

Sutter Home Winery's Frē

Sutter Home would like you to forget all you just read about cold filtration. They don't believe in it. Instead, they've put their money, and their dealcoholized wine, on the spinning cone.

Developed and widely used in Australia, the spinning cone is a two-stage process that removes the essence of the wine before the alcohol is removed. Wine is fed into the top of a spinning cone column—a cylinder roughly forty inches in diameter and thirteen feet in height. The wine flows from the top, down over a series of metal cones as neutral nitrogen gas is injected at the bottom of cone. The gas carries the aroma and flavor from the wine. These wine essences are put aside, and the process is repeated at higher temperatures to remove the alcohol. The essences are then reunited with the liquid, and blended with unfermented varietal grape juice. The nectar of the gods meets stainless steel.

Why does this make it better? "We feel it's the superior technology," says Hock. "Aromas and flavors, the essences, are removed and safeguarded. It's fresher and more like wine."

Sutter Home jumped into the nonalcoholic market in 1993 with the national release of a chillable light red White Zinfandel and a Chardonnay. "We'll come out with a red Frē and a sparkling Frē," says Hock. Sutter Home produces approximately 200,000 cases per year.

Other Wineries

Other wineries, smaller wineries, and importers have jumped into the fray, betting on the expanded market. Doug Welsch at Fenn Valley Vineyards began his research and experimentation in 1985, and seriously started to market his nonalcoholic wines in the Midwest and Canada in 1990.

Wineries exist in more than thirty-five states. Guidebooks

such as the *Guide to American Vineyards*, by Pamela Stovall, or *Vintage Places*, by Suzanne Goldenson, offer a list of local wineries. Some of them, like Fenn Valley Vineyards, may be producing excellent nonalcoholic wine in your own neighborhood.

Sales

The market for dealcoholized wine has exploded from a mere several thousand cases in the mid-1980s, to 500,000 to 600,000 cases in 1994.

Fenn Valley's Welsch says his sales started jumping in 1992 and 1993. "Before, it was an unknown beverage category and an unknown product, so it was doubly hard to move the wine. The United States had a negative image of 'non' anything. We've ridden on the coattails of nonalcoholic beer. It's more understood now."

Other producers of dealcoholized wine expect, and hope, that the upward trend will continue, agreeing with Welsch that the acceptance of nonalcoholic "beer" has expanded the market for their product. Analysts predict that in the next few years the market could expand to several million cases per year.

Prices

Dealcoholized wines run the full range of prices. Some are more economical than wine with alcohol, and others are sold at a comparable price or higher. The product is also offered with a cork or screw cap.

Sparkling Juices

The outcasts, according to dealcoholized winemakers, are juices masquerading as nonalcoholic wine. The juice in these bottles has never been fermented, and it is sweet because the sugar has not been consumed during fermentation. Some of these juices are quite palatable and make a refreshing nonalcoholic beverage. Some are made from the juices of native American grapes, such as Concord and Niagara. New to the sparkling juices market is the use of varietal grapes, such as Chardonnay and Pinot Noir. If you don't expect a champagne taste, many of these sparkling juices, without added sugar and sold in a champagnelike bottle, offer a great alternative to alcoholic champagne for any festive occasion.

Serving Dealcoholized Wine

Much of the enchantment of wine comes from the ceremony of "experiencing wine," shared with friends. Go ahead and serve dealcoholized wine with all the pomp and pedantry of wine with alcohol. Sniff the cork. Murmur comments about how it's an impudent year but will soon grow mellow, or say that it has the nose of the varietal but not its finish.

Treat dealcoholized wines just as you would their with-alcohol cousins. Chill whites and rosés in the refrigerator or a champagne bucket. Care should be given that the wine glasses are free of spots and soap. Fill the glass only one third to half full so there's room to swirl the wine, releasing all the pleasant fragrances.

Dealcoholized wine is best served with a meal when entertaining both people who usually drink wine with alcohol and those who usually drink wine without. The food helps to mask the lighter "mouthfeel" of the wine.

Another option is to use dealcoholized wine for spritzers or coolers, made as if you were using wine with alcohol.

Serve dealcoholized sparkling wine as you would champagne, in a flute or champagne glass. Sparkling wines are fabulous at a party because everyone may participate in a festive toast and feel part of the party. And isn't that what every host or hostess strives for?

Meier's

Cranberry Chablis

4 ounces cranberry juice
4 ounces Meier's
 nonalcoholic Sparkling
 Chablis

1. Fill a tall glass with ice.
2. Pour in juice and Chablis.
3. Stir well.

CALORIES: 132

Orange Blossom

3 ounces orange juice
3 ounces Meier's
 Sparkling Catawba
 Grape Juice

1. Chill a tulip champagne glass.
2. Pour well-chilled orange and grape
 juice into champagne glass.
3. Stir.

CALORIES: 84

Catawba Cocktail

4 ounces Meier's
 nonalcoholic Catawba
 Grape Juice
4 ounces ginger ale

1. Fill a tall glass with ice.
2. Pour in grape juice and ginger ale.
3. Stir.

CALORIES: 104

Ohio's largest and oldest winery, Meier's has been making wine and bottling grape juice for more than one hundred years. John C. Meier planted vines in Ohio in the 1850s. Perhaps his greatest success at the time was a process he invented at the turn of the century to keep juice fresh long after it was pressed from the grapes. The grape juice soon traveled the country to thirsty buyers. Today, Meier's is known for its quality grape juices, sparkling grape juices, and wine. Meier products were served at the White House in 1979 during the signing of the Israel-Egyptian peace agreement. Meier's offers samples of its products at the tasting bar at the winery near Cincinnati.

Opus One
Classic Kir

1 drop grenadine
2 ounces Clearly
  Canadian raspberry
  sparkling water
3 ounces Ariél
  Dealcoholized
  Sparkling wine
1 lemon twist

1. Place one drop of grenadine in the bottom of a 6-ounce champagne glass.
2. Add raspberry sparkling water.
3. Top glass with sparkling wine.
4. Garnish with a lemon twist.

CALORIES: 38

The new Motown sounds are the rumblings of happy tummies. Chef Peter Loren smokes all his meats, poultry, and seafood; bakes the bread; whips up the sauces; and concocts the desserts, all on site, for his American cuisine with a French flair. No wonder Opus One, in Detroit, has won so many honors: the city's 1993 restaurant of the year, by *Detroit Monthly* magazine; and two Five Star Diamond Awards in 1991, as one of the top fifty continental restaurants and as one of the top fifty restaurants in the U.S.

Top of the Mark
Breath-a-Lizer

1 splash cranberry juice
1 glass nonalcoholic wine

1. Pour a splash of cranberry juice into a wine glass.
2. Fill glass with nonalcoholic wine.

CALORIES: 25 or higher, depending on the wine you choose.

With an address like One Nob Hill, the Mark Hopkins Inter•Continental is the place to be in San Francisco. The hotel's nineteenth-floor penthouse, opened in 1939 as the glass-walled Top of the Mark lounge, provides a 360-degree view of the San Francisco Bay Area. The Top of the Mark gained a worldwide reputation during World War Two when hundreds of thousands of Allied servicemen shipped through San Francisco, and many used it as the real port of embarkation. Today, bartender Bert Rees uses the view for inspiration ... for great new drink ideas.

The Ritz-Carlton, Buckhead
Grape Juice Cocktail

5 ounces chilled Riesling grape juice (Chablis or Chardonnay grape juice may be substituted)
1 dash puree of currants (raspberries may be substituted)
1 mint leaf

1. Pour Riesling grape juice into a white-wine glass.
2. Add dash of puree of currants.
3. Garnish with a mint leaf.

CALORIES: 125

Every day, Chef Guenter Seeger issues a new handwritten menu for The Dining Room at the Ritz-Carlton, Buckhead, in Atlanta. A typical evening's scribbles might include bass in port wine and red beet sauce and a boffo Jamison farm lamb on black truffle potato tart. It's no wonder that the restaurant has received the AAA Five Diamond Award for five consecutive years. The dining room boasts silk upholstered seating, flower arrangements, and oil paintings from the eighteenth and nineteenth centuries.

The Greenbrier Old White Club

Virgin Bellini

1½ ounces chilled peach juice

4 ounces chilled Ariél nonalcoholic sparkling wine

Spiraled lemon peel

1. Pour the chilled peach juice into a champagne flute.
2. Add the sparkling wine.
3. Garnish lip of champagne flute with spiraled lemon peel.

CALORIES: 75

Historic doesn't begin to describe The Greenbrier, in Sulphur Springs, West Virginia. People visited in the 1700s to "take the waters," to cure any and all ailments. After the Civil War, Old White, as the resort was called, became the summer home of General Robert E. Lee. In the winter of 1941–1942, the "guests" of The Greenbrier were German and Japanese diplomats that the United States government wasn't quite sure what to do with. Later during the Second World War it became an army hospital. After the war the hotel was completely redecorated. Twenty-two United States presidents have visited the resort. And duffers such as Arnold Palmer, Bob Hope, and Bing Crosby have putted on the resort's three courses. Swimming, great dining, horseback riding, trout fishing, and tennis are available, as well as mineral baths, which originally put Sulpher Springs on the map.

The Milton Inn
Raspberry Cooler

14 large fresh raspberries
3 ounces soda water
1 ounce simple syrup
Crushed ice
3 ounces nonalcoholic
    Regina Champagne
Mint leaf for garnish

1. Place all but one of the large fresh raspberries, the soda water, and simple syrup in a blender.
2. Puree.
3. Fill a Collins glass with crushed ice.
4. Pour pureed mixture into the Collins glass.
5. Top with Regina nonalcoholic Champagne.
6. Garnish with raspberry and mint leaf.

CALORIES: 187

Gourmet magazine called the Milton Inn "the favorite haunt of the jodhpur set," and its kitchen "the best in the state." Near Baltimore in Sparks, Maryland, the Milton Inn resides in a 240-year-old fieldstone building. In years past, it has been a coach stop for Quakers, the Milton Academy, and a school for boys named in honor of poet John Milton; one alumnus was John Wilkes Booth, President Abraham Lincoln's assassin. Since 1947, it has been home to an inn where fine dining and nonalcoholic beverages may be enjoyed in a candlelit dining room or on the open-air garden terrace.

The Pursuit of Hoppiness

A Guide to Domestic and
Imported Nonalcoholic Beers

For all of the hoopla that has greeted the recent emergence of nonalcoholic brews—or NAs—as a growing market, it should be noted that, sixty-five years ago, NAs had the market all to themselves. Among the best-selling legal beers during Prohibition were Anheuser-Busch's Bevo, Miller's Vivo, Stroh's Luxo, Schlitz's Famo, and Pabst's Pablo, Hoppy, and Yip. The fact that these brands appeared to be named after forgotten Marx brothers and Disney dwarves did little to help their appeal. What truly hurt them, however, was that they were a poor substitute for real beer.

It is not surprising, then, that the airwaves are not cluttered with commercials for Bevo Draft or Pablo Light. Brewers abandoned their NAs at a moment after midnight on the day Prohibition was repealed and, for the most part, tried to forget the whole business. The closest a major brewery came to a relapse occurred in 1984, when Anheuser-Busch trailed Miller and its top-ranked Lite by a vast margin in the light beer craze, and decided to take the less-is-more trend a step further, though not all the way to zero-proof. A-B introduced its L.A. low-alcohol beer with a relentless marketing campaign; unfortunately, the product itself was a bland, watery disappointment, even though it contained six times more alcohol than today's NAs.

It's hard to say what has transpired since then to make the NA category the fastest-growing market segment, but certainly a few factors are influential: the increased emphasis on physical fitness, tougher laws against drunken driving, and a social stigma about drinking to excess. Women, whose consumption of beer has increased since the introduction of light beers, have turned to nonalcoholic alternatives during pregnancies. There's also been an improvement in the taste of American NAs, and a better supply of imports. And perhaps one psychological factor is a key. For the first time, brewers have labeled their NAs with names that sound like

135

real brands of beer: Sharp's, O'Doul's, Cutter, Texas Select, and so on.

Drinkers of nonalcoholic brews now have a range of options. Some of the NAs are truly outstanding, and can hold their own with the best alcohol-laden beers the world's breweries have to offer. Many others are reasonably acceptable substitutes for beer.

Though NAs are snubbed by beer connoisseurs, they are gaining respect where it counts: in supermarkets, restaurants, and bars. While NAs account for just 1.5 percent of the brewing industry's total sales, they are swelling at a time when the market for traditional beers is flat. In 1991, sales of NA brews rose by 32 percent, while the total beer category increased by less than 3 percent. In 1992, overall beer sales showed no increase, but NA sales shot up another 32 percent, to 72 million barrels. Brewing industry experts forecast that NAs will account for 10 percent of all beer sales by the end of the decade.

Pushing that growth upward will be the muscle of the brewing giants: Anheuser-Busch, Miller, and, to a lesser extent, Stroh's and Coors. Their prowess in production, distribution, and marketing allows the big breweries to roll out millions of barrels while shelling out millions of dollars in advertising. Their involvement also brings credibility in the minds of consumers. For example, research done by Coors found that, in late 1989, before the big brewers became involved, consumers couldn't tell the difference between NA brands, the brews were perceived as poor-tasting, and NA drinkers were seen as people who switched to the products for health reasons.

A study done a few months later, after Miller introduced Sharp's and Anheuser-Busch debuted O'Doul's, revealed that consumers were more aware of NAs, the taste of the brews was perceived as better, and NA drinkers were considered to be health-conscious, rather than unhealthy.

In 1992, Coors sponsored another study, following the

introduction of its Cutter label. The brewery found that consumers were accepting NAs as a mainstream product line, could distinguish among the various brands, and were purchasing them more regularly. Most significantly, NA drinkers were seen as people who were just as normal as other beer drinkers. Perceptions aside, the typical NA drinker has an average household income of $40,000 or more, is male (57 percent), and is slightly older than the average beer drinker (50 percent of NA drinkers are between the ages of 25 and 44). When Stroh's introduced its NA in selected markets in late 1993, the brewery targeted an even older audience: consumers aged 30 to 49.

These changes in the image of NAs are good news to the big brewers, and their new, higher profile provides a benefit to consumers: NAs now are available in thousands of stores, restaurants, and bars, for the first time. The drawback, though, is equally significant: Since O'Doul's and Sharp's hit the market, the imports have rapidly lost favor. Within three years, their share slid from a third of the category to 5 percent.

More significantly, the smaller, more creative regional brands have suffered. Firestone and Fletcher, a California microbrewery that focused exclusively on making nonalcoholic beer, was a casualty of the NA boom. In 1990, its Firestone brew outsold the fifteen bottled beers at Eureka, Wolfgang Puck's brewery/restaurant in Los Angeles. A couple of years later, it had vanished. A Firestone and Fletcher official says the company pulled the plug despite growing sales because its competition had changed. A few years ago, only a handful of NAs were available. Today it seems as if every brewing company has started touting its own boozeless brew.

At last count, the number of brands available in the U.S. exceeded seventy, and many more are being tested. The top ten brands enjoy 93 percent of NA sales, led by O'Doul's, with 31 percent of the market, and Sharp's, with 29 percent.

When choosing a nonalcoholic brew the key issue is not, of

course, how many barrels the brewery sells, though this will determine how easy it is to find. What really matters are the answers to two questions: How does it taste? And, more to the point, how closely does the flavor resemble real beer?

Many newspapers and magazines have conducted blind taste competitions to answer those questions. Because there are no absolutes in what a beer should taste like, it is impossible for one group of individuals, whether they are brewing industry experts, bartenders, journalists, or barflies, to rank them in a way that is meaningful to the subjective palate of anyone else. There is also a risk that factors can bias the perceived taste of a brew in a single comparison in one location: regional taste preferences, a city's climate, the temperature of the room, the temperature of the beer, the freshness of the samples, and so on.

For this reason, we conducted our own blind taste comparison, in which we rated the five best-selling domestic and five best-selling imported brews. Without exception, the highest rankings were awarded to imports: Haake-Beck, Clausthaler, Buckler, St. Pauli NA, and Kaliber finished first through fifth.

We then compared our findings with the results of several tests conducted by panels from a diverse array of publications in various regions:

The ten highest rankings in the *Chicago Tribune*'s tasting went to NAs that were brewed overseas or in Canada. In descending order, they were St. Pauli NA, Haake-Beck, Molson Exel, Moussy, Stades, Buckler, Kaliber, Clausthaler, Warsteiner, and Thomas Brau.

The *Cincinnati Post* graded NAs on a scale of A through F. The imports Buckler and Kaliber received As; Moussy and Sharp's rated Bs; and O'Doul's, Molson Exel, St. Pauli NA, and Cutter were graded as Cs.

Mademoiselle magazine's top seven NAs were imports— Molson Exel, Buckler, Moussy, Clausthaler, Haake-Beck,

Kaliber, and Zero Plus. The remaining five brews rated were all American brands.

The *Washington Post* deemed that only two brews, Buckler and St. Pauli NA—both imports—were of "good" quality; Haake-Beck, Clausthaler, Coors Cutter, and Molson Exel fit into the "acceptable" range; Moussy, Kaliber, Sharp's, and O'Doul's were of "fair" quality; and "poor" ratings went to Kingsbury, Carling's Black Label NA, and Pabst NA.

A *Consumers Digest* panel bestowed four stars on Clausthaler, Kaliber, Ziegel Hof, Haake-Beck, and Gerstel, all of which are imported. Buckler, Birell, Cutter, and St. Pauli NA rated three stars. Two stars, the lowest rating given, went to Black Label, Kingsbury, Moussy, O'Doul's, Old Milwaukee, Sharp's, and Texas Light—except for the Swiss-made Moussy, all were brewed in the U.S.

These results confirmed our own impressions: The clear winners in head-to-head tastings are imports. The difference is in the brewing methods, which we'll review a bit later. For people who enjoy full-bodied beers, the sweet aromas and weak flavors of American NAs are a disappointment. Many of them taste like light beers that have been further diluted with water. But for those who have tried only these brands, the robust flavors of the imports below will seem a revelation.

Buckler, from Heineken (Holland), offers a sweet aroma, fine gold color, dry finish, and a rich head that leaves a lacelike residue as the glass is emptied. It would sell even better if marketed as Heineken Light.

Clausthaler, from Binding (Germany), boasts a pale amber color, a powerful aroma, and a strong, bitter finish.

Exel, by Molson (Canada), delivers a malty fragrance, a full-bodied flavor, and a well-balanced finish.

Haake-Beck, from Dribeck (Germany), pours out in a honey color with a creamy head, a malty bouquet, and a dry finish reminiscent of Beck's.

Kaliber, from Guinness (Ireland), makes an impression with

a rich head, light amber color, strong malt notes, a slightly watery mouth, and balance at the finish.

St. Pauli NA, from St. Pauli (Germany), provides a luminous gold hue crowned by a thick head, and a balanced finish with lingering hops.

One American NA was introduced too recently to be included in the newspaper and magazine taste competitions cited above. We found that, even with a couple of flaws, it nearly measured up to the imports.

Royal Amber, by G. Heilemann (U.S.) presents a faint trace of hops in the nose, deep mahogany hue, thicker head than other domestics, slightly fruity flavor, and a somewhat watery finish.

Despite their poor showing in many tastings, it's worth remembering that the top-selling NAs are those made by Anheuser-Busch and Miller. Why would these brands prove so popular at the retail level, but finish near the bottom in taste tests? For one thing, A-B and Miller benefit from brand loyalty: A Bud drinker switching to an NA will reach for an O'Doul's; a Miller Lite loyalist will opt for a Sharp's. And, of course, these labels are heavily advertised and widely available. The taste, in other words, is not the only factor that NA buyers consider, even though they may be shortchanging themselves.

In fairness, there is another possibility: The judges in a taste competition may try more than a dozen NAs in a single sitting, and the samples that stand out will be those that make the strongest flavor impressions. A rich, bitter taste, however, may not be what a typical NA drinker desires. On a humid afternoon, or after an exhausting racquetball game, a bland, watery beer is more refreshing than a hop-heavy import.

Nor does it hurt that domestic beers are priced at about 40 percent less than the cost of imports. This difference in price matters because, surprisingly, most nonalcoholic brews cost more than traditional beers. This would seem to suggest that the consumer is paying more for a product that offers less. If the brewery removes the alcohol, why doesn't it charge a lower price? Unfortunately, that isn't the way it works in Milwaukee and on Madison Avenue.

First, the NA market is a relatively new one, and, despite its rapid growth, accounts for a mere 1.5 percent of the multibillion dollar brewing industry. Advertising, packaging, and the brew itself cost more per bottle because the product is made in smaller quantities. This is reminiscent of the early years of the low-calorie light beer segment, when the initial higher costs led to steeper prices for the consumer. But here's a bonus that consumers overlook when comparing prices among brews in a supermarket cooler: If they buy an NA, they will not be burdened by a hefty sin tax at the register. NAs are legally exempted from the alcohol tax.

But the major reason why NAs cost more is because the methods used to brew without alcohol, or to remove the alcohol after fermentation, are more expensive than traditional brewing processes. Brewers can use one of four methods to create malt beverages without alcohol. The first two are used primarily in the United States, and both result in a loss of beer flavor. The third and fourth processes, used in making imports, are more expensive techniques that allow the brew to keep nearly all of the taste characteristics of real beer. But each of the methods below is more costly than brewing beer with alcohol.

• **Heat:** As anyone who has baked a rum cake knows, alcohol evaporates when heated. Because water evaporates at a higher temperature than does alcohol, American brewers use this technique to slowly heat the beer until the alcohol is removed. The problem with this approach is that the ingredients that most enhance the flavor of beer—malt and hops—are weakened as well.

• **Vacuum evaporation:** In this process, the beer is fully fermented, and then placed in a vacuum, where less heat is needed to evaporate the alcohol. The lower temperature allows the brew to hold more of its flavor than a brew that is made using the heat method alone. The top-selling import, Kaliber from Ireland's Guinness brewery, uses this method.

• **Dialysis:** After fermenting, the beer is filtered through a membrane through which only the alcohol molecules can pass. A variation on this method is called reverse osmosis, in which pressure is added to push the beer against the membrane. Most of the German NAs are made in this way.

• **Smart yeasts:** Developed in Switzerland, these genetically engineered yeasts stop the fermentation process just before alcohol is produced. They're commonly called "dumb yeasts" in the brewing trade, but the truth is that these strains are anything but underachievers. So far, only the Swiss are using this approach, because none of the other breweries is willing to pay the royalty fees.

Whichever method is used, the Federal Bureau of Alcohol, Tobacco & Firearms requires that all products sold as nonalcoholic brews contain less than half of 1 percent of alcohol by volume. Most NAs, however, are actually well below the limit; Pabst NA's alcohol content by volume is 0.14, and the full-bodied import Kaliber is just 0.2. This means that one could drink 150 bottles of Kaliber, or 214 bottles of Pabst NA, before imbibing the amount of alcohol in a six-pack of a typical American lager, which contains 5 percent alcohol by volume. And, because trace amounts of alcohol are produced naturally in many products, more booze is present in two slices of whole-grain bread, in 12 ounces of lemon-lime sodas such as 7-Up, or in 12 ounces of freshly squeezed orange juice, than exists in a nonalcoholic brew.

Low alcohol levels translate into low calories. The average beer with alcohol, domestic or import, contains 150 calories per 12-ounce can. Light beers typically contain about 98 calories per can. A 12-ounce glass of orange juice has 162 calories; Pepsi, 150; 7-Up, 141; tonic water, 132; ginger ale,

132. Now consider the number of calories in 12 ounces of the NAs that are most widely available in the United States:

UNITED STATES		FRANCE	
Coors Cutter	76	Tourtel	69
Goetz	65		
Kingsbury	60		
NA (made by Pearl)	55	GERMANY	
Old Milwaukee NA	72	Haake-Beck	96
O'Doul's	70	Clausthaler	96
Pabst NA	55	St. Pauli NA	101
Royal Amber	60		
Sharp's	58		
Stroh's NA	72	HOLLAND	
Texas Select	71	Buckler	75
AUSTRALIA			
Swan Special Light Lager	60	IRELAND	
		Kaliber	71
CANADA			
Labatt .5	80		
Molson Exel	74	SWITZERLAND	
Northern Goose	60	Birell	78

With the exception of the German NAs, all of the brews listed above contain fewer calories than the immensely popular light beers. But, due to the reduction in calories and alcohol, one characteristic is lacking in all NAs: the sensation of fullness in the stomach that a beer with alcohol brings. While this can seem a bit unsettling at first—swallowing a light beer has, in fact, been compared to drinking wet air— because of this, NAs provide a perfect complement to meals, offering full flavor without the heavy feeling that reduces the appetite.

Even the best brews will lose their flavor if not handled properly. This is especially true of NAs, because they lack the higher concentrations of alcohol that preserve the freshness of real beer. Here are some guidelines to ensure that your nonalcoholic brew reaches your table with all of the taste characteristics that the brewmaster intended.

Avoid buying beer from stores that do a sluggish business in NA sales, and never purchase beer long before it will be used; in both instances, beer goes stale after a few months. If the beer is encoded with a freshness date, check to see that it has not expired. For example, the labels of Haake-Beck and Clausthaler include grids of months and years; notches made at the brewery indicate when the brew will pass its peak. Though few other breweries follow this practice, you can look at the Haake-Beck labels even if you are buying another brand to glean how well the retailer rotates his stock: If the fresher Haake-Beck bottles are found in the back of the display, the same is probably true of the other brews. But, if the older stock is in the back, you'll know that the retailer is continuously placing new shipments in the front, while allowing the older product to grow stale. Also, stay away from any malt beverage that is displayed in a store window or in a lighted cooler—exposure to light spoils beer, whether it contains 5 percent alcohol or 0.5.

When you bring the brew home, store it immediately in a dark, cool place, with the tops of the bottles or cans facing up. Placing the beer on its side allows the liquid to mix with the air at the top of the container, and results in a stale taste.

Serve the brew in the vicinity of 40 to 45 degrees Fahrenheit. Clean glasses are a must—dishwashing detergents can leave a film that stifles the head, and for this reason, some aficionados insist that soap suds should never be used to clean beer glasses. Instead, try sterilizing them in the rinsing and high-heat drying cycles of a dishwasher.

The glasses used for drinking NAs, naturally, should be classic beer glasses: pilsner flutes, heavy mugs with handles, 12-ounce hourglasses, Irish pub pints, or skyscraping Weiss beer vessels.

Now tilt the glass, and pour the beer in a slow, even stream against the inner side. Just after the bottle is emptied, straighten the glass to allow the head to form with a flourish.

Don't take a sip yet. First, give garnishes a try. Beer drinkers with a hankering for the hearty taste of a Weiss beer will find that a slice of lemon adds flavor and an acidic complement to the taste of an NA. Squeeze the juice from the lemon into the foam, then drop the rind into the glass. Or mimic the experts: At the Hotel Inter•Continental's Top of the Mark lounge in San Francisco, bartender Bert Rees is beloved for his habit of topping a glass of nonalcoholic brew with a splash of Rose's lime juice, a concoction he calls a Check Point Chandy.

Now you're ready for the smooth, satisfying taste of a well-made brew. As you savor the taste, remember that the best nonalcoholic brews can deliver everything that you love about a traditional beer, and then some. Lower calories, and lower alcohol, mean that you can enjoy drinking as many NAs as you want tonight—and tomorrow, instead of a throbbing headache, what you'll have to show for it is a vivid, very pleasant memory.

Douglas Dunes Sir Douglas Cafe

Bull Shot

3 ounces Bloody Mary
    mix
6 ounces nonalcoholic
    brew (beer)
1 lime slice

1. Fill a large glass with ice.
2. Pour the Bloody Mary mix into the glass.
3. Add the brew.
4. Garnish with lime.

CALORIES: 66

Located in West Michigan, the Saugatuck-Douglas area is a haven for Chicago and Detroit tourists who flock to the former artists' colony for its unique shops and beautiful, sandy, Lake Michigan beaches. Douglas Dunes is a popular resort featuring rooms and cottages, an excellent restaurant, and six bars, ranging from a loud-and-crazy bar with dance music to the quiet lounge by the pool.

Setting Up
Your Own
Nonalcoholic Bar

You're organizing your first home bar. Or maybe you're adding only a few elements. Either way, this chapter will brief you on everything you'll need at home to make exceptional drinks without alcohol.

Utensils for the Bar

Basic tools of the trade can make your life as a bartender easier.

Blender
Can opener—one with a fang that opens large juice cans
Chopping board
Coasters
Cocktail shaker—one with a strainer and lid
Corkscrew
Fruit knife
Ice bucket
Juicer—whether electric or manual
Lemon squeeze
Lemon squeeze

Measuring cup
Measuring spoons
Mixing glass
Mixing spoon—a long handled spoon for stirring and measuring ingredients
Shaker cup
Shot glass
Strainer—to remove ice, or lime and lemon seeds
Straws
Stirrers
Tongs and ice scoop
Toothpicks, cocktail skewers

Juices

Great drinks begin with fresh ingredients. This holds true especially with juices. However, for those times when an impromptu party may occur, cans, bottles, or concentrate will save the day. Keep some handy just in case.

Cranberry juice
Grapefruit juice
Orange juice

Pineapple juice
Tomato juice

Mixers

Don't give in to the temptation of just pouring a cola and considering it a nonalcoholic drink. With the following mixers on hand, you'll always be ready to entertain.

Cola
Ginger ale

Sprite or 7-Up
Soda

Mixes

Manufacturers have responded to those who don't care to drink alcohol by creating new and delicious mixes. Many, such as Bloody Marys or daiquiris, may be poured as is.

Bacardi has introduced new Frozen Concentrated Tropical Fruit Mixers, in flavors such as Margarita and Strawberry Daiquiri. For a frozen drink, combine the mixer with ice in a blender. Each package yields five 8-ounce drinks. Skip the blender for a cold beverage on the rocks.

Nonalcoholic wine or beer can be used as a mixer, for spritzers or bull shots, or served as is. These two items alone will satisfy most visitors.

Simple Syrup

To make simple syrup, mix 2 cups of water with 2 cups of sugar in a saucepan. Heat mixture almost to boiling point. Continue heating until mixture is reduced to approximately 2 cups. Store in a cool place.

Ingredients

The following ingredients are basics to have on hand for the nonalcoholic bar.

Bar salt for margaritas
Bitters

Celery salt
Grenadine

Honey
Lemon juice
Lime juice
Pepper
Rose's lime juice

Salt
Sugar
Tabasco
Worcestershire sauce

Garnishes

Whoever said presentation is everything was right—especially for drinks. A lemon swirl, a cherry, or chocolate shavings not only make the drink look good, but also make it taste better. A well-stocked bar will have the following garnishes.

Cherries
Chocolate to be shaved
Lemons

Limes
Oranges
Pineapple

Glassware

Much like garnishes, the right glass helps the bartender present the drink well. The basic glasses are the highball, Collins, wine, champagne flutes, margarita, and beer mug. Additional ones to fill the bar are goblets, old-fashioned, poco grande, and champagne dish.

Make sure your glasses are free of soap spots, and chill or frost them before guests arrive. Fill them with solid ice, not with ice that's melting.

If you know in advance that you'll be having guests, special ice cubes can add a certain flair. Frozen fruit juice cubes will keep juice-based drinks from becoming too diluted. Also, you can add food coloring or pieces of fruit or mint in the cubes for a special presentation.

Glossary and
Guide to Measurements

Measurements

1 dash	=	1/4 ounce if sweet, 1/8 ounce if bitter
1 teaspoon or barspoon	=	1/8 ounce
3 teaspoons	=	1 tablespoon
2 tablespoons	=	1 ounce
1 shot	=	1 ounce
1 jigger	=	1 1/2 ounces
4 tablespoons	=	1/4 cup
16 tablespoons	=	1 cup
1 cup	=	8 ounces
2 cups	=	1 pint
4 cups	=	1 quart

Glossary

Cooler: Similar to a punch, but with less citrus juice; usually calls only for rinds of lemons or oranges. Unlike a punch, which is served in a large bowl with fruit, a cooler is a well-iced summer drink served in a tall glass.

Flag: A type of garnish in which the fruit is presented in a distinctive manner. The most common variety is the orange/

153

cherry flag, in which a cherry is centered in an orange slice, through which a skewer is placed.

Frappé: A drink poured over cracked ice in a cocktail glass.

Frozen: A drink that is mixed in a blender with ice.

Mix: Vigorously stir the ingredients until they blend to a uniform color and consistent texture.

Mixing glass: Used for most cocktails that call for fruit juices. It should hold at least 16 ounces and have a pouring spout.

Salt rim: Rub a lime wedge around the rim of the glass. Then turn the glass upside down on a dish covered with salt.

Shake: Liquids that are not clear usually need to be shaken to combine them sufficiently. Using a container with a lid, shake the mixture in a back-and-forth or an up-and-down motion.

Shaker cup: Used for combining non-carbonated liquids (soft drinks tend to foam). Usually stainless steel, the shaker consists of three parts: a cup into which the ingredients are poured; a cup-shaped lid that is placed over the contents before they are shaken; and a strainer that removes seeds and pulp as the drink is poured into a glass.

Stir: Most clear liquids need only to be stirred. Gently move a spoon or swizzle stick through the liquid in a circular motion. Carbonated beverages should be stirred as little as possible to prevent foaming.

Up or **neat:** Strain out the ice and pour the drink into a glass that does not contain ice.

Glassware

STEMWARE

Sour
glass

Goblet/
Water glass

Red wine
glass

White wine
glass

Bloody Mary
glass

Hurricane/
Squall glass

Frappé/Parfait
glass

Margarita/
Daiquiri glass

Martini
glass

Brandy
snifter

155

Champagne
dish

Champagne
flute

Champagne
tulip glass

Pilsner/Beer
glass

BARWARE

Highball/Up/
Tumbler/Soda
glass

Iced Tea/
Zombie glass/
Irish Pub
pint glass

Collins/Chimney/
Tall/Soda
glass

Old-fashioned/
Rocks glass

Beer mug

156

Index of Drinks by Name

160

Geographic Index

ALASKA

Juneau

The Fiddlehead
429 West Willoughby Avenue
Juneau, AK 99801
Tel: (907) 586-3150

ARIZONA

Carefree

The Pool Pavilion
The Boulders Resort
34631 North Tom Darlington
P.O. Box 2090
Carefree, AZ 85377
Tel: (602) 488-9009

Grand Canyon

Bright Angel Lodge
Box 699
Grand Canyon, AZ 86023
Tel: (602) 638-2631

Phoenix

Vincent Guerithault on Camelback
3930 East Camelback Road
Phoenix, AZ 85018
Tel: (602) 224-0225

Tucson

The Tack Room
2800 North Sabino Canyon Road
Tucson, AZ 85715
Tel: (602) 722-2800

ARKANSAS

Little Rock

Juanita's
1300 S. Main Street
Little Rock, AR 72202
Tel: (501) 372-1228

CALIFORNIA

Anaheim

Disneyland Hotel
1150 W. Cerritos Avenue
Anaheim, CA 92802
Tel: (714) 778-6600

Beverly Hills

The Bar
The Regent Beverly Wilshire
9500 Wilshire Boulevard
Beverly Hills, CA 90212
Tel: (310) 275-5200

Coronado (San Diego)

Palm Court Lounge
Hotel del Coronado
1500 Orange Avenue
Coronado, CA 92118
Tel: (619) 435-6611

Los Angeles

Hotel Bel-Air
701 Stone Canyon Road
Los Angeles, CA 90077
Tel: (310) 472-1211

L'Orangerie
903 N. La Cienaga Boulevard
Los Angeles, CA 90069
Tel: (310) 652-9770

Spago
8795 Sunset Boulevard
West Hollywood, CA 90069
Tel: (310) 652-3706

Pebble Beach

Lobby Bar
Inn and Links at Spanish Bay
2700 Seventeen Mile Drive
Pebble Beach CA 93953
Tel: (408) 647-7500

The Tap Room
Lodge at Pebble Beach
Cypress at Seventeen Mile Drive
Pebble Beach CA 93953
Tel: (408) 624-3811

San Francisco

Fog City Diner
1300 Battery Street
San Francisco, CA 94111
Tel: (415) 982-2000

Tonga Room & Fairmont Hotel
950 Mason Street
San Francisco, CA 94106
Tel: (415) 772-5000

John's Grill
63 Ellis Street
San Francisco, CA 94103
Tel: (415) 986-0069

Peer Inn
Pier 33
San Francisco, CA 94111
Tel: (415) 788-1411

Stars
150 Redwood Alley
San Francisco, CA 94102
Tel: (415) 861-7827

Top of the Mark
Mark Hopkins Inter•Continental
One Nob Hill
San Francisco, CA 94108
Tel: (415) 392-3434

COLORADO

Aspen

Restaurant at The Little Nell
675 E. Durant Avenue
Aspen, CO 81611
Tel: (303) 920-6330

Denver

The Buckhorn Exchange
1000 Osage Street
Denver, CO 80204
Tel: (303) 534-9505

Strings
1700 Humboldt Street
Denver, CO 80218
Tel: (303) 831-7310

Colorado Springs

The Rendezvous Lounge
Broadmoor Hotel
1 Lake Avenue
Colorado Springs, CO 80906
Tel: (719) 634-7711

DELAWARE

Wilmington

Green Room
Hotel Du Pont
11th and Market Streets
Wilmington, DE 19899
Tel: (302) 594-3154

DISTRICT OF COLUMBIA

Gerard's Place
915 15th St., N.W.
Washington, DC 20005
Tel: (202) 737-4445

Hawk 'n' Dove Restaurant
329 Pennsylvania Avenue S.E.
Washington, D.C. 20003
Tel: (202) 543-3300

Town & Country Lounge
Stouffer Mayflower Hotel
1127 Connecticut Avenue N.W.
Washington, D.C. 20036
Tel: (202) 347-3000

Vidalia
1990 M Street N.W.
Washington, DC 20036
Tel: (202) 659-1990

Potomac Lounge
The Watergate
2650 Virginia Avenue N.W.
Washington, D.C. 20037
Tel: (202) 965-2300

FLORIDA

Key West

Louie's Backyard
700 Waddell Avenue
Key West, FL 33040
Tel: (305) 294-1061

Old Havana Docks Lounge
The Pier House Resort &
  Caribbean Spa
1 Duval Street
Key West, FL 33040
Tel: (305) 296-4600

Fort Lauderdale

Mai-Kai
3599 North Federal Highway
Fort Lauderdale, FL 33308
Tel: (305) 563-3272

Miami

Grand Cafe & Ciga Lounge
The Grand Bay Hotel
2669 S. Bayshore Drive
Coconut Grove, FL 33133
Tel: (305) 858-9600

Hotel Inter-Continental
100 Chopin Plaza
Miami, FL 33131
Tel: (305) 577-1000

Mark's Place
2286 Northeast 123rd Street
North Miami, FL 33181
Tel: (305) 893-6888

Palm Beach

The Breakers
Alcazar Lounge
One South County Road
Palm Beach, FL 33480
Tel: (407) 655-6611

Palm Beach Gardens

Waterway Cafe
2300 PGA Boulevard
Palm Beach Gardens, FL 33410
Tel: (407) 694-1700

St. Lucie

Club Med's Sandpiper Village
3500 Morningside Boulevard
Port St. Lucie, FL 34952
Tel: (407) 335-4400

GEORGIA

Atlanta

Buckhead Diner
3073 Piedmont Road
Atlanta, GA
Tel: (404) 262-3336

The Dining Room at The
  Ritz-Carlton
Buckhead
3434 Peachtree Road
Atlanta, GA 30326
Tel: (404) 237-2700

Pricci
500 Pharr
Atlanta, GA 30305
Tel: (404) 237-2941

Resto des Amis
3060 Peachtree Road
Atlanta, GA 30305
Tel: (404) 364-2170

HAWAII

Honolulu

Michel's
The Colony Surf Hotel
2895 Kalakaua Avenue
Honolulu, HI 96815
Tel: (808) 923-5751

ILLINOIS

Chicago

Bossa Nova
1960 North Clybourn
Chicago, IL 60614
Tel: (312) 248-4800

Kingston Mines
2548 N. Halsted Street
Chicago, IL 60614
Tel: (312) 477-4646

Lee's Unleaded Blues
7401 S. South Chicago Avenue
Chicago, IL 60619
Tel: (312) 493-3477

The Marc
311 W. Superior Street
Chicago, IL 60610
Tel: (312) 642-3810

Mother's
26 West Division
Chicago, IL 60610
Tel: (312) 642-7251

Planet Hollywood
633 North Wells
Chicago, IL 60610
Tel: (312) 266-7827

Sage's Sages
75 W. Algonquin Road
Arlington Heights, IL 60005
Tel: (708) 593-6200

Second City
1616 North Wells Street
Chicago, IL 60614
Tel: (312) 337-3992

Wish's
2834 North Southport Avenue
Chicago, IL 60657
Tel: (312) 281-4833

LOUISIANA

New Orleans

Hilton Riverside
Kabby's Sports Edition
Two Poydras Street
New Orleans, LA 70140
Tel: (504) 584-3880

Pat O'Brien's
718 St. Peter Street
New Orleans, LA, 70116
Tel: (504) 525-4823

MARYLAND

Baltimore

Haussner's
3244 Eastern Avenue
Baltimore, MD 21224
Tel: (410) 327-8365

Sparks (Baltimore)

The Milton Inn
14833 York Road
Sparks, MD 21152
Tel: (410) 771-4366

MASSACHUSETTS

Back Bay (Boston)

Daisy Buchanan's
240a Newbury Street
Back Bay, MA 02116
Tel: (617) 247-8516

Boston

Biba
272 Boylston Street
Boston, MA 02116
Tel: (617) 426-7878

Cambridge

The House of Blues
96 Winthrop Street
Cambridge, MA 02138
Tel: (617) 491-2583

Stockbridge

The Red Lion Inn
Main Street
Stockbridge, MA 02162
Tel: (413) 298-5545

MICHIGAN

Detroit

Doug's Body Shop
22061 Woodward
Ferndale, MI 48220
Tel: (313) 398-1940

Opus One
565 East Larned
Detroit, MI 48226
Tel: (313) 961-7766

The Rattlesnake Club
300 River Place
Detroit, MI 48207
Tel: (313) 567-4400

Grand Rapids

GR Steamer Bar
Charley's Crab
63 Market S.W.
Grand Rapids, MI 49503
Tel: (616) 459-2500

Douglas

Sir Douglas Cafe
Douglas Dunes
333 Blue Star Highway
Douglas, MI 49406
Tel: (616) 857-1401

Mackinac Island

Jockey Club at The Grand Stand
The Grand Hotel
Mackinac Island, MI 49757
Tel: (906) 847-3331

MISSOURI

St. Louis

Tony's
410 Market Street
St. Louis, MO 63102
Tel: (314) 231-7007

Webster Groves
Big Sky Café
47 S. Old Orchard Road
Webster Groves, MO 63119
Tel: (314) 962-5757

NEW HAMPSHIRE

Hanover

The Ivy Grill
Hanover Inn at Dartmouth College
Wheelock & Main
Hanover, NH 03755
Tel: (800) 443-7024

NEW MEXICO

Santa Fe

The Cactus Rose at Rancho
  Encantado
Route 4
Box 57C
Santa Fe, NM 87501
Tel: (505) 982-3537

Old House Restaurant
Eldorado Hotel
309 West San Francisco Street
Santa Fe, NM 87501
Tel: (505) 988-4455

NEW YORK

Montauk

Gosman's
500 West Lake Drive
Montauk, Long Island, NY 11954
Tel: (516) 668-5330

New York City

The Blue Bar
The Algonquin Hotel
59 West 44th Street
New York, NY 10036
Tel: (212) 840-6800

CBGB & OMFUG
315 Bowery
New York, NY 10003
Tel: (212) 982-4052

Daniel
20 E. 76th Street
New York, NY 10021
Tel: (212) 288-0033

Queen Elizabeth 2
Cunard
555 Fifth Avenue
New York, NY 10017
Tel: (800) 221-4770

Fantino
The Ritz-Carlton
112 Central Park South
New York, NY 10019
Tel: (212) 664-7700

The Four Seasons
99 East 52 Street
New York, NY 10022
Tel: (212) 754-9494

The Rainbow Room
30 Rockefeller Plaza
New York, NY 10112
Tel: (212) 632-5100

Sardi's Restaurant
234 West 44 Street
New York, NY 10036
Tel: (212) 221-8440

S.O.B.'s (Sounds of Brazil)
204 Varick Street
New York, NY 10014
Tel: (212) 243-4940

The '21' Club
21 West 52nd Street
New York, NY 10019
Tel: (212) 582-7200

NORTH CAROLINA

Pinehurst

Ryder Cup Lounge
Pinehurst Resort & Country Club
P.O. Box 4000
Pinehurst, NC 28374
Tel: (910) 295-8436

OHIO

Cincinnati

The Maisonette
114 E. 6th Street
Cincinnati, OH 45202
Tel: (513) 721-2260

Meier's Wine Cellars, Inc.
The John C. Meier Co.
6955 Plainfield Pike
Cincinnati, OH 45236
Tel: (513) 891-2900

Cleveland

Piperade
123 West Prospect Avenue
Cleveland, OH 44115
Tel: (216) 241-0010

OREGON

Portland

Jake's Famous Crawfish Restaurant
401 South West 12th Avenue
Portland, OR 97205
Tel: (503) 226-1419

Key Largo Restaurant & Bar
31 North West 1st Avenue
Portland, OR 97209
Tel: (503) 223-9919

PENNSYLVANIA

Philadelphia

The Swann Lounge
The Four Seasons Hotel
One Logan Square
Philadelphia, PA 19103
Tel: (215) 963-1500

RHODE ISLAND

Providence

Oliver's Review
83–85 Benevolent Street
Providence, RI 02906
Tel: (401) 272-8795

SOUTH CAROLINA

Hilton Head Island

The Westin Resort
Two Grasslawn Avenue
Hilton Head Island, SC 29928
Tel: (800) 228-3000

Myrtle Beach

Dixie Belle Saloon
Dollywood Entertainment Park
P.O. Box 7507/8901-B
Highway 17 Business
Myrtle Beach, SC 29577
Tel: (803) 497-6615

TENNESSEE

Pigeon Forge

Dixie Belle Saloon
Dollywood Entertainment Park
P.O. Box 58/3849 Parkway
Pigeon Forge, TN 37868
Tel: (615) 453-9473

TEXAS

Austin

Antone's
2915 Guadalupe Street
Austin, TX 78705
Tel: (512) 474-5314

Dallas

The Mansion Bar
The Mansion on Turtle Creek
2821 Turtle Creek
Dallas, TX 75219
Tel: (214) 559-2100

Houston

Cafe Annie's
1728 Post Oak Blvd.
Houston, TX 77056
Tel: (713) 840-1111

Fitzgerald's
2706 White Oaks
Houston, TX 77007
Tel: (713) 862-7580

Four Seasons Hotel
1300 Lamar Street
Houston, TX 77010
Tel: (713) 650-1300

San Antonio

The Landing
Hyatt Regency Hotel
123 Losoya
San Antonio, TX 78212
Tel: (210) 223-7266

UTAH

Salt Lake City

The Bay
404 S. West Temple Street
Salt Lake City, UT 84101
Tel: (801) 363-2623

Snowbird

Lodge Club
Lodge at Snowbird
Snowbird, UT 84092
Tel: (801) 742-2222

VIRGINIA

Richmond

The Frog & The Redneck
1423 E. Cary Street
Richmond, VA 23219
Tel: (804) 648-3764

Washington

The Inn at Little Washington
Box 300
Middle and Main Streets
Washington, VA 22747
Tel: (703) 675-3800

Williamsburg

Williamsburg Inn
136 E. Francis Street
Williamsburg, VA 23185
Tel: (800) 447-8679

WASHINGTON

Seattle

Kaspar's
2701 First Avenue
Seattle, WA 98121
Tel: (206) 441-4805

The Painted Table
The Alexis
1007 First Avenue at Madison
Seattle, WA 98104
Tel: (206) 624-4844

Top of the Needle Lounge
The Space Needle Restaurant
219 4th Avenue N.
Seattle, WA 98109
Tel: (206) 443-2100

WEST VIRGINIA

White Sulphur Springs

Old White Club
The Greenbrier
White Sulphur Springs, WV 24986
Tel: (800) 624-6070

WISCONSIN

Kohler

The Horse and Plow
The American Club
Highland Drive
Kohler, WI 53044
Tel: (414) 457-8888

Blackwolf Run Clubhouse
Blackwolf Run Golf Course
Kohler, WI 53044
Tel: (414) 457-4448

Milwaukee

Karl Ratzsch's Old World
   Restaurant
430 E. Mason Street
Milwaukee, WI 53202
Tel: (414) 276-2720

Sanford Restaurant
1547 N. Jackson Street
Milwaukee, WI 53202
Tel: (414) 276-9608

Plymouth

52 Stafford
52 Stafford Street
P.O. Box 217
Plymouth, WI 53073
Tel: (414) 893-0552

WYOMING

Jackson Hole

Granary Lounge
Spring Creek Resort
1800 Spirit Dance Road
Jackson Hole, WY 83001
Tel: (800) 443-6139

dozen magazines and newspapers, including *Playboy, Us, Chicago, Outside, The Chicago Tribune*, and *Spy*.

He also has written extensively about nightlife, including a profile of Chicago's "hot" night spots for *Rolling Stone*. His feature about nonalcoholic drinks, "Drinks for the Designated Driver," was published in *Playboy*.

He lives in Chicago with his wife, Margaret, and daughter, Megan.